1

# 90 to Nothing

## A Devotional for the Busy Soul

## By

## Karen Mutchler Allen

# Dedication

This book is dedicated to my precious mama, Kathy Mutchler.

I've watched you spend time with your Savior my entire life. Kneeling with your open Bible beside you. Calling out our names before the Father. Journaling. Worshiping. Loving. You have set before me an example of what it looks like to walk with God and for that, I am forever grateful. I love you mama!

# Day 1

"But Martha was distracted by all the preparations
that had to be made." Luke 10:40

Distracted. Busy. Pre-occupied. Harried. Any of
these words sound like a description of **your** day?
Martha could identify. She was preparing her
house to entertain guests and boy was she busy.
Martha, the busy bee. Buzzing all around to get
everything done. She looks around to enlist the
help of her sister and she doesn't find her
mopping…or dusting…or cooking. Instead, she
finds her *sitting*. I can imagine Martha gasping at
the picture of her sister *sitting* when in her mind,
Mary should be *serving*. But see, Mary wasn't
sitting on the couch taking a nap or watching TV
or even playing on her phone. Nope…she was
sitting at the feet of Jesus, listening to Him talk.
She was soaking in the presence of Jesus. Waiting
with baited breath to hear what He might say to
her. I can imagine that all the mopping in the
world wouldn't have stolen a minute of her
attention…not when Jesus was there, sitting in her
living room. Guess what? This is why I was
drawn to write this devotional. We are so busy

going "90 to nothing", busy as a bee, with so much stuff to get done that we don't stop…and Jesus is in our living room. Or our office. Or our kitchen. He's waiting for that moment where we say, "I need to catch my breath, Lord…I need to sit at your feet. What will you say to me today?" We need a "Selah" moment…which means to pause and "think of that". What is "that"? Well, "that" is whatever Jesus is talking to *you* about. Whatever He shows you in His Word. Whatever He reveals to your heart. Pause and think of that. When we are hurried, rushed, and busy, we forfeit the chance to sit at His feet, hear what He has to say, and "Selah". Some of you are like Martha…there are things to be done, goals to be met, calls to be made, people to manage, and you must do it all. There is no time to be lazy or unproductive. So, you just go, go, go…until you can't go anymore, right? I'm thankful for the "Martha's" of the world…you get stuff done…but don't forget that it is necessary to take the time to spend with Jesus. Uninterrupted, purposed, time with Him…even if it's just for a few moments. Guess what Jesus said about Mary's time at his feet? He said, "Mary has chosen what is better, and it will not be taken away from her." See, it wasn't Martha's immaculate home or scrumptious meal Jesus was after. He was after her heart. *Selah*.

Question of the day: Do you relate to Martha and if so, how does this devotion speak to you?

Quote of the day: "Shut the world out, withdraw from all worldly thoughts and occupations, and shut yourself in alone with God, to pray to Him in secret. Let this be your chief object in prayer, to realize the presence of your heavenly Father." Andy Murray

Prayer: Jesus…I've been too busy, too distracted, too hurried and I have not made time to sit at your feet. Help me balance the desire I have inside to be busy and productive at all cost, with the desire I have to spend time with You. I know there are things You want to tell me and I want to hear them, Lord. I really do. Help me to Selah. Thank You for loving me enough to remind me to slow down and spend time with You. I love You. I ask this in Your Son's precious Name, Amen.

Further Scripture Reading:

Luke 10:38-42

# Day 2

"And the God of all grace, who called you to his eternal glory in Christ, after you have suffered a little while will himself restore you and make you strong, firm, and steadfast." 1 Peter 5:10

Suffering is not on my list of things to do today, or any day for that matter. No one, and I mean no one LIKES to suffer. It is NEVER on our agenda is it? But, reality is, suffering happens to all of us at some point in our lives. Not because WE are bad or terrible or have done something wrong but because this world is broken and we live in it. I so often wish I could skip over the suffering part just like I skip over all the previews in a movie. Or like I skip over all the directions when I'm putting a desk together. You know, just skip it. Suffering is painful, exhausting, uncomfortable, and it never feels like it leaves fast enough. Suffering happens in many forms and looks different for every person. You may want me to tell you that once you come to know Jesus, you will not suffer. I can't. But what I can tell you is that when you *do* suffer, God Himself will restore you. He will lovingly rub the Balm of Gilead over the places

that have been wounded.  He will speak to the
open gashes that suffering left behind.  Know
what else?  Not only will God Himself restore you,
but He will make you strong, firm, and steadfast.
So, suffering, as hard as it is, will bring forth
healing and restoration from God Himself as well
as providing you with His strength which is firm
and steadfast.  I never WANT to suffer but when I
do, I know I don't suffer alone and there will be
something beautiful that comes from my suffering.
Rest in that truth today, Dear One.

Question of the day:  How does this change the
way you see suffering?

Quote of the day:  "Suffering has been stronger
than all other teaching, and has taught me to
understand what your heart used to be.  I have
been bent and broken, but – I hope – into a better
shape."  Charles Dickens

Prayer:  God, you know I don't like to suffer.  I
don't like to suffer for a short period of time or
even worse, a long period of time.  But the truth is,
I know suffering will come my way and I trust

You to see me through it, tend to my wounds, restore me, and give me your strength so I will be firm and steadfast in my journey. Thank you for not letting me suffer alone. You are so, so, good to me. I love you. I pray this in Jesus Name Amen.


Further Scripture Reading:

Job 36:15

Romans 5:3

# Day 3

"And if you leave God's paths and go astray, you will hear a voice behind you say, "No, this is the way; walk here." Isaiah 30:21 (TLB)

You can ask anyone who really knows me and they will agree that I'm what you would call, "Directionally Challenged". I could get lost in my own backyard. I wouldn't be able to find my way out of a paper sack. I have a severe case of "geographical dyslexia" and will easily admit to having a "directional disability". I've been lost more times than I can count and if my gut tells me to turn right, I have now learned to utterly dismiss my gut feeling and just turn left. I don't know why directions are so hard for me, but they are. One time I was driving to speak at a conference in the mountains and my cell lost all service. Jesus take the wheel. I had no idea how to get to where I was going. I just kept driving, all the while hoping to see giant billboards saying, "Karen, this is the right way!" or "Karen, turn left ahead!" Did I? Nope. Not one stinkin' sign. I finally got to the conference but it was because I had to pull over and ask someone who was just going to "tell" me how to get there. I laughed at that man and said, "Sir, you're going to need to write that down please!" Life is full of directions, isn't it? Do we turn right or left? Do we take this path or that one? What if we started in the right direction but took a wrong turn. What if we started in the wrong direction but now we are headed in the right one? Whew, it's so confusing sometimes, isn't it? In our Christian walk, we may not have large billboards with our name on it or a GPS commenting in a British accent that we have gone the wrong way, but we do have a map. And not only do we have a map, but we belong to the One who WROTE the map. God's Word is full of directions. Directions that point us toward the right path and how we should live. At times, we may take a right when we should have taken a left and the ultimate GPS provider, God Himself, will say, "No, this is the way, walk here." I'm so thankful that He has given us the Bible to direct us but when we get off track as sometime we will, we can be assured that He will speak to us and remind of us the right direction. His path. His road. The one that leads Home.

Question of the day: Have you ever gotten off-track in your walk with Christ and if so, how did God bring you back?

Quote of the day: "The greatest honor is the right direction one is turned into by the Holy Spirit." Sunday Adelaja

Prayer: Abba, I know I need to rely on You for the direction of my life. Decisions and directions are so hard and sometimes I go the wrong way. When I do, please help me to hear Your voice as You direct me in the right way to go. Whether it is through Your Word or Your direct voice, help me to follow Your directions because they are always good and they are always right. My desire is to go the direction You want me to go in because I know that You will never steer me wrong. I can never be lost if I'm following You. Thank You Lord. I ask this in Jesus Name, Amen.

Further Scripture Reading:

Psalm 32:8

Isaiah 48:17

# Day 4

"As a dog returns to his vomit, so a fool repeats his folly." Proverbs 26:11

Before you get married, I believe there are some important things you should know about how this whole "two-become-one" thing works. Like, where does your future spouse squeeze the toothpaste tube? Or, will he/she take the trash out when it's full or wait for it to overflow? Will they pick up after themselves once they've cut their toenails or leave them all scattered on the couch? Now, there is one item that should absolutely be decided before marriage...who cleans up the throw-up. That's right, throw-up. Vomit. Yack. Puke. Tossing your cookies. Whatever you call it, it's downright disgusting and I detest cleaning it. Whether it's mine, his, the kids, or the dogs...I.just.can't. In fact, I dare say they should change the sound of the morning alarm to a dog yacking because nothing makes me get up faster than that sound! Speaking of dog puke, have you ever had a dog throw up and then eat it? You haven't lived until you've experience that little piece of heaven. I have to admit the only thing good about that is at least then, there is less yack for me to clean up. Well, whether we want to admit it or not, we can be just like those vomit-eating dogs when we keep repeating a mistake over and over again. It's one thing to make a mistake, it's another thing to continue making that same mistake repeatedly. The Bible calls us FOOLS when we do this! Listen, every one of us will mess up because, well, let's face it, we're human. Mess-ups, mistakes, or poor decisions will happen to all of us, no doubt. That's not the issue here. The issue here is when we make a mistake, **know** it is a mistake, and still continue to do it. It's as stupid as a dog eating its own vomit. Own your mistake and move on. Don't be a fool and make the DECISION to continue *choosing* that same mistake. Why? Because it's gross to eat your own throw-up. Really gross.

Question of the day: Have you ever made the same mistake over and over again and if so, what good came from it?

Quote of the day: "You never make the same mistake twice. The second time you make it, it is no longer a mistake, it is a choice" Lauren Conrad

Prayer: Lord, I don't want to keep making the same mistakes over and over again. Please give me the strength to overcome that desire. Help me to recognize the mistake and then move on. I don't want to be a fool in Your eyes. I love you and am thankful for the grace I have when I do make a mistake. I pray this prayer in the powerful Name of Your Son and my precious Savior, Jesus. Amen.

Further Scripture Reading:

Hebrews 10:26

1 John 3:9

# Day 5

"Religion that God our Father accepts as pure and faultless is this: to look after orphans and widows in their distress and to keep oneself from being polluted by the world." James 1:26

I don't follow a religion.  I am not religious either. What?  You're probably thinking, "Ummm...Karen...this is a DEVOTIONAL...you MUST be religious!"  Nope.  Not me.  See, we've somehow linked "Religion" to rules, judgements, and staunch traditions.  When I read the above verse all I see is PEOPLE.  Look at it again.  Do you see it now?  People.  The religion that God is talking about revolves around people.  People are the point.  Being religious isn't about the "knowing", it's about the "loving".  Knowing the Ten Commandments doesn't make me religious. Loving the unlovable does.  Understanding that Jesus died on the cross for our sin doesn't make me religious.  Sharing that life-changing Truth with people does.  God loves people.  He sent His Son to save people.  Remember, people are the point.  I don't ever want to be known for my religion. I want to be known for how I love His people.

Question of the day: How does James 1:26 change your view of "Religion"?

Quote of the day: "The Church exists for nothing else but to draw men into Christ, to make them little Christs. If they are not doing that, all the cathedrals, clergy, missions, sermons, even the Bible itself, are simply a waste of time. God became Man for no other purpose." C.S. Lewis

Prayer: Oh Father God, how I've missed it sometimes! You don't want or need me to be religious. You don't care about my religion either. You care about people. Please forgive me for missing this truth at times. Help me to remove religion and replace it with a deep love for You and Your precious people. May I never equate religion and rules with the power of the truth. That truth is LOVE. May I love like You love and may it break every curse of religion in the powerful Name of Jesus of Nazareth, Amen.

Further Scripture Reading:

Luke 10:25-37

# Day 6

"If we claim to be without sin, we deceive ourselves and the truth is not in us. If we confess our sins, he is faithful and just and will forgive us our sins and purify us from all unrighteousness."
1 John 1:9

"I'm sorry. Please forgive me." my husband said to me one day. It has always amazed me at how well he does that. He's not afraid of the "I'm Sorry's". He's not intimated by the task of asking for forgiveness. He is usually the first one to say it when we have had "an intense moment of communication" which is just a fancy way to say we had a fight! Me, on the other hand, well, I'm not so great at it. Those words get stuck in my throat. They taste like a mixture of mud and motor oil. I don't like to admit when I am wrong but I'm the first to bring attention to when I've *been* wronged…nice huh?! I've learned in my walk with God that the "I'm Sorry's" don't have to be so terrible. God is not standing in Heaven with His arms crossed, tapping His foot, with an irritated look on His face waiting for me to say I'm sorry for something. It's not a newsflash to Him

22

that I'm a sinner. He knows it and longs to forgive me when I ask. So, I say, "God, I'm sorry for (fill in the blank). Please forgive me." and usually before I even get those words out of my mouth, I hear His voice speak these beautiful and redemptive words, "You are forgiven." God makes the "I'm Sorry's" easy and I am so grateful for that...I really don't like the taste of mud and motor oil.

Question of the day: How often do you ask God for forgiveness for your sins?

Quote of the day: "The ability of a person to atone has always been the most remarkable of human features." Leon Uris

Prayer: Father, thank You for being approachable when I need to ask for forgiveness for something. You make it so easy to say, "I'm Sorry". You are always ready to extend forgiveness and pour grace and mercy over me. Help me to come to You when I've sinned and have grieved Your heart. Allow my spirit to quickly recognize when I need to come to You for forgiveness and help my spirit to accept Your complete forgiveness as well. Thank you Father! I ask this in Your Son's Holy and Powerful Name, Amen.

Further Scripture Reading:

Psalm 130:3-4

Ephesians 1:7-8

# Day 7

"The LORD remembers us and will bless us…he will bless those who fear the LORD –small and great alike." Psalm 115:12-13

I forgot my kid once. Yup. Had to turn around and go get her. At least I *remembered* that I had *forgotten*, right? Do you feel forgotten sometimes? Like maybe the big God of the entire universe doesn't remember that you exist? Or like maybe He doesn't remember creating you and so He never really thinks about you? Well, Beloved, let me just tell you, He remembers you. And not only does He remember you, but He will bless you. Maybe not with a bazillion dollars or a Porsche, but He will bless you. And His remembering you and blessing you doesn't hinge on what you do…because it says "small and great alike". You don't have to be a "pastor of somewhere" or a "president of something" to be remembered by God or to be blessed by Him. You're His child. And yes, sometimes certain mom's forget their children at the ballfield, but God doesn't. He can't. He won't. He remembers you and longs to bless you. And now you can be thankful that I'm not your mama…because you'd need to hitch a ride.


Question of the day:  Does God remember you?

Quote of the day:  "God bestows His blessings without discrimination." F.F. Bruce


Prayer:  Lord, thank You for remembering me and wanting to bless me.  On the days I feel forgotten, I ask that you would bring this verse to my mind and heart and remind me of this Truth!  I can't be forgotten because I am Yours.  You WILL remember me and You WILL bless me and I receive those blessings in Jesus Name.  I love you and I am thankful for Your heart for me.  I pray this prayer in Jesus Name, Amen.

Further Scripture Reading:

Isaiah 49:15-16

Romans 10:12


Worship:  10,000 Reasons by Matt Redman

# Day 8

"I will listen to what God the LORD says..." Psalm 85:8

I remember sharing a story with Lindsey while we were dating and I said, "The Lord told me "such-and-such". He furrowed his brow, cocked his head to the right and sat there with a very quizzical look on his face. He never said anything that day but years later he shared with me that every time I said that phrase (and I said it often) he had a hard time wrapping his mind around it. The fact that I "heard the Lord" the way that I did was really strange to him which was strange to me! I began to understand that I heard the Lord speak to me in one way and Lindsey heard him in another. Neither one of us was wrong. God isn't so small that there is only one way for Him to speak. In Exodus 3, God spoke to Moses through a burning bush. In 1 Kings 19, Elijah heard God in a gentle whisper. In Luke 1, God spoke to Mary through the angel Gabriel. In Numbers 22, God spoke to Balaam using a donkey. Yup, a donkey! It's time for us to quit thinking we all need to hear God speak to us in the exact same way. He made us unique and the way He will speak to our hearts will mirror that. He can use nature, other people, circumstances, His Word, music, and a multitude of other ways to speak to you. Don't worry if you don't hear Him like me and I won't worry that I don't hear Him like you. We are His sheep. We will listen to His voice. We will follow Him.

Question of the day: How do you hear God's voice?

Quote of the day: "God isn't so small that there is only one way for Him to speak." Karen Mutchler Allen

Prayer: Father, thank You for Your voice! Help my heart to always recognize it and never compare how You speak to someone else. You created me uniquely and that is how You will speak to me as well. I love to hear Your voice and I love You! I pray this in Jesus Name, Amen.

Further Scripture Reading:

1 Samuel 3

# Day 9

"When Jesus reached the spot, he looked up and said to him, "Zacchaeus, come down immediately, I must stay at your house today." Luke 19:5

I almost missed it. Almost. The cashier behind the counter began beeping my items. I was busy trying to calm my young son in the front of the cart, because, well, let's face it, he was all done with being at the grocery store. This visit came on the heels of a visit where I actually left my entire cart of items and exited the store because my little dude had an absolute meltdown. So, I was feeling the pressure, you know, the "I only have about twelve more minutes before the volcano erupts…" kind of pressure. I was distracted and in a hurry and wasn't really feeling the need to engage anyone at this point. I just wanted to get out of the store as quickly as possible with a happy child and all my groceries. But, I felt Him. I felt Him nudge my heart. I really wasn't sure what I was supposed to do next so I just looked at the cashier and said, "How are you today?" She looked at me and her jaw just hung open. She finally said, "Wow, no one has ever asked ME how I'm doing...it's usually the other way around." I laughed and then told her that she mattered and that she was important. She opened up, began to pour out her struggles. I told her I'd be praying for her and at those words, she began to cry. And to think I almost missed it. When Jesus was walking through Jericho that day, he was just passing through. I'd imagine he was tired, and dirty, and just wanted to get where he was going. But Jesus was so intentional when it came to people and relationships. He stopped at a sycamore tree, looked up, and told Zacchaeus to come down because they were going to eat dinner together. That intentionality on Jesus' part changed Zacchaeus' life forever. Jesus didn't walk around with his head in the clouds OR in the sand. He walked around with the sole purpose of interacting with people in order to change their life. Intentional living and intentional loving. Don't miss it.

Question of the day: How can you be more intentional today?

Quote of the day: "An unintentional life accepts everything and does nothing. An intentional life embraces only the things that will add to the mission of significance". John C Maxwell

Prayer: Father God, help me to be intentional today. Help me to look for where You want to work through me. Show me when I need to stop and really pay attention to someone or to something. Help me to look for those Zacchaeus' in a tree, call them down, and eat dinner with them. People matter to You. I don't want to miss it, God, not today. I love You and I ask this in the beautiful Name of Jesus, Amen.

Further Scripture Reading:

Luke 19:1-9

# Day 10

"Jesus replied, "Anyone who loves me will obey my teaching. My Father will love them, and we will come to them and make our home with them." John 14:23

I had a little bit of a difficult time obeying when I was a little girl. Please don't ask my parents to elaborate...because they will...a bunch. Let's just say I struggled with the rules. And obeying them. I remember one time I was heading outside to play and my mama reminded me not to go in the road. Well, I didn't just go *in* the road, I sat on the yellow line. I got a spanking. A very B.I.G. one. Obeying did not come easy to me. I didn't like being told what to do. Still don't. Obedience doesn't really come natural to anyone...just ask a mom of a three year old. The thing is, obedience is necessary as it recognizes authority but I find that my pride is a stumbling block to obedience. In my walk with the Lord I have found that because I love Him, I choose to obey what He says. Please note that I did not say "want", I said "choose". Obedience is a surrender of the will for the purpose of trusting that God IS faithful. He never asks us to obey without there being a reason. Now, we may not understand the reason or even get to know what that reason is in our lifetime, but obedience is the "action" of trusting Him. Obedience to God is a direct reflection of trusting Him to be who He says He is and to do what He says He'll do. Obedience isn't easy sometimes but it's always worth it…just ask my mama.

Question of the day: How does obeying God show your trust in Him?

Quote of the day: "God is God. Because he is God, He is worthy of my trust and obedience. I will find rest nowhere but in His holy will that is unspeakably beyond my largest notions of what he is up to." Elisabeth Elliot

Prayer: Father, I trust You and love You and because I do, I choose to obey You. When I have the choice to obey or disobey, please help me remember that You are always faithful and that You are for me. You want what is best for me and are always on my side and because of that, I know You are worthy of my obedience. I believe that obedience to You is a direct reflection of my trust IN You. I love You, Abba, and I pray this prayer in Your precious Son's Name Jesus, Amen.


Further Scripture Reading:

Deuteronomy 28:1-2

1 John 2:5-6

# Day 11

"They sow the wind and reap the whirlwind."
Hosea 8:7

There's a story in the Bible that has always haunted me. The story is about a man named Achan and it's found in Joshua 7. Joshua, captain of the Israelite army, gave specific instructions to conquer Jericho. His soldiers were to kill every single person in the city and they were not to keep any of the plunder. All of the silver, gold, articles of bronze and iron, were considered sacred and were to go into the Lord's treasury. Achan was one of Joshua's soldiers and he decided to steal a beautiful robe from Babylonia, two hundred shekels of silver and a wedge of gold weighing fifty shekels. He took them and hid them in the ground inside his tent. Joshua didn't know that Achan had gone against his demands and stolen the sacred items. He then sent his army to fight a weaker army but to his horror, the army Joshua had sent was defeated. Some of his soldiers died during what was supposed to be an easy win for Joshua. Joshua went to the Lord, desperate for answers. The Lord revealed that there was sin in the camp and it needed to be dealt with. Once Achan confessed, Joshua took Achan, his sons, his daughters, his cattle, donkeys, sheep, his tent and all that he had and brought them to the Valley of Achor where all of Israel stoned and burned them. Did ya'll read that? *All* of Achan's family died. *All* of them. Can you see now why this story is a tough one to swallow? **Achan** sinned…not his sons, not his daughters, not even his sheep. But they all paid the price for *his* sin. Achan sowed the wind…but he reaped the whirlwind. Sometimes we get more than we bargained for when it comes to sin. Our sin can affect others. It cost Achan's family their life. I use to think that one person's sin wouldn't affect another person…this story proves that to be wrong. And so does the story of a husband cheating on his wife. They divorce and the children are broken. Who paid for that sin? And so does the story of a drunk driver hitting a family of four, killing three of them. Sin doesn't just affect the one who does the sinning. You may sow the wind but you must also be ready to reap the whirlwind.

Question of the day: In your opinion, how did Achan sow the wind but reap the whirlwind?

Quote of the day: "When men sow the wind it is rational to expect that they will reap the whirlwind." Frederick Douglass

Prayer: Oh Father God, so many times I have been guilty of thinking that my sin will only affect me. Please forgive me for all the times that my sin caused other people hurt, brokenness, and pain. I do not want to sow the wind and reap the whirlwind. I'm thanking You in advance for helping me see this truth. Thank You, Lord, I ask this in Jesus Name, Amen.

Further Scripture Reading:

Joshua 6 and 7

# Day 12

"Reckless words pierce like a sword, but the tongue of the wise brings healing." Proverbs 12:18

"Sticks and stones may break my bones but words will never hurt me!" We've all heard that at one time or another, haven't we? But the truth is, that's a lie. A big fat lie actually. Words, especially if they are reckless, hurt deeply. And just like toothpaste squeezed from a tube that cannot be returned, reckless words act in the same manner. Once they are released, they cannot be returned…ever. Forgiveness can be asked and received but the damage is done. I was thinking of how choosy I am with what I wear and what shoes I put on my feet but I am reckless with my words, throwing them around without consideration. If it takes me several minutes to decide what pair of jeans to wear, shouldn't it take me more than a second or two to choose what words will come out of my mouth? We can't be reckless with a car, or a gun, or someone else's life and neither can we be reckless with our words. Our words matter because people matter. Reckless words are worse than sticks or stones could ever be.

Question of the day: Can reckless words really cause damage?


Quote of the day: "Handle them carefully, for words have more power than atom bombs." Pearl Strachan Hurd


Prayer: Father God, I don't want to use words that pierce, hurt, or destroy. Reckless words do not have a place on my lips because I know they are a mirror to what is in my heart. Help me to stop and think before I use words that could hurt or maim others. I want my words to be healing and full of hope. I'm asking You today to do a work in me and I believe You for it in Jesus Name, Amen.


Further Scripture Reading:

Proverbs 16:24

Ephesians 4:29

# Day 13

"He who walks with wise men will be wise, but the companion of fools will suffer harm." Proverbs 13:20 (NAS)

There's an old saying that says, "You are what you eat!" which would be hilarious to see a bunch of candy bars walking around, or maybe a bag of chips, possibly a big juicy steak or maybe every now and then a carrot or an apple. Well, we both know that we don't actually become what we eat, but did you know that we **do** become like the people we are around? Motivational speaker Jim Rohn famously said that we are the average of the five people we spend the most time with. This relates to the law of averages, which is the theory that the result of any given situation will be the average of all outcomes. So, write down the five people you spend the most time with. Assign each person with a numerical value from 1~10 which indicates how much influence they have in your life (with 10 the most influence possible). Who has the most influence of the five? Who has the least? Are these five people making you better? Are they challenging you to be the best you? This doesn't mean they are "yes" people, just telling you what you want to hear, it means they tell you what you NEED to hear, even if it's difficult to say. Are these five people investing in you? Are they helping you to become wise? Take a minute out of your day today to thank those that made this list in helping you become the best version of you. If there is someone on your list that isn't the best influence, think about how to lessen that person's influence in your life. You don't want to be a bag of chips when you could be a Filet Mignon.

Question of the day: Do you agree or disagree with Jim Rohn's thoughts? Why or why not?

Quote of the day: "Surround yourself with the dreamers, and the doers, the believers, and thinkers, but most of all, surround yourself with those who see the greatness within you, even when you don't see it yourself." Edmund Lee

Prayer: Father, thank you for the names on my list. Thank you for their investment in me and helping me to become the person You are creating me to be. Bless them, encourage them, and speak to their hearts today Lord.  If there is a person on that list that has great influence over me but it is not the kind of influence You desire, show me how to lessen his/her influence in my life. Help me to walk with the wise so I may continue to grow wise and may I always be quick to recognize when I need to change the list of influencers. Thank You, Father, for Your provision of these great influencers and may I be a great influencer for them as well.  I pray this in the strong Name of Jesus, Amen.


Further Scripture Reading:

Proverbs 27:17

1 Corinthians 15:33

# Day 14

"But if I say, "I will not mention him or speak any more in his name, his word is in my heart like a fire, a fire shut up in my bones. I am weary of holding it in, indeed, I cannot." Jeremiah 20:9

Have you ever known an important piece of information but you weren't able to share it with anyone else? Didn't you feel like you would just burst? I remember finding out we were pregnant for the first time and I wanted the whole world to know. Even though I wanted to tell EVERYONE, I also felt like I needed to go to the doctor first just to be sure! The wait time between when I found out I was pregnant until the doctor confirmed it felt like a stinkin' lifetime. I NEEDED to tell people…all the people…any of the people…even the people I didn't know. Everyone needed to hear our news! Why? Why did I feel like that? Well, because I was excited! Excited at the news. Excited with the possibilities. Excited with it *all*. Jeremiah knew what this felt like. Not the being pregnant part, but the part of being so excited about something he couldn't contain it, he couldn't hold it in. God's Word was in him like a fire and it was just burning to get out! This speaks of a passionate desire to know God's Word and for it to cause a fire, so much so that it HAS to come rushing out. We speak about what we are passionate about, don't we? It doesn't take long when speaking with someone to know what they are passionate about and what they love. I believe whole-heartedly that if I had the opportunity to speak to Jeremiah, I would know quite quickly Who he was passionate about. Would Jeremiah say the same about you?

Question of the day: What are you passionate about?

Quote of the day: "If you want to discover the true character of a person, you have only to observe what they are passionate about." Shannon L. Alder

Prayer: Father, create in me the passion for You and for Your Word like Jeremiah had. The kind that goes to my bones. I want to be passionate about You...so much so that I cannot hold it all in. I want the love I have for You to come out in my speech, my actions, and my character. Be the fire inside my veins. Let nothing compare to the desire I have for You. Light me up from the inside out and help me burn for You. I trust You for it, I believe You for it, in Jesus Name, Amen.

Further Scripture Reading:

Jeremiah 15:16

Romans 12:11


Worship: King of my heart by Sarah McMillan

# Day 15

"Do not judge, or you too will be judged. For in the same way you judge others, you will be judged, and with the measure you use, it will be measured to you." Matthew 7:1-2

"She has tattoos, piercings, and a Mohawk?" YIKES! Would you let your son date a girl like that? Well, that girl is ME! Yup! I didn't always have tattoos, piercings, and a Mohawk but I do now...and it's wonderful. Wanna know why? I'll give you one word...freedom. Somewhere down the line, Christians believed a lie and that lie is, "If you don't look like me, talk like me, or do things like I do them, you are wrong and I have the right to judge you." You don't have the right. Neither do I. We don't have the right to judge a hairstyle, an outfit, the way someone worships, what they eat, what they drive, or anything else that isn't a *sin*. We have made our personal preferences universal principles. We.are.wrong. You may not like long hair on guys but it isn't a sin and so when they sit next to you in church and you make a judgement about them, it's you who has sinned. You may not like the loud worship music that is played in some churches.  That's okay.  That's your preference.  The problem comes when you make a judgement in your heart about the people who *do* like it.  When we make judgments based on our preferences, we take God out of the equation. *Sin* is to be judged, not whether or not we agree with ripped jeans in church or not.  Honestly, if I were to be judged solely on my appearance, I probably wouldn't be let in most churches.  And that would be a shame.  Not because I'm anything but because God can use me for His glory...tattoos and all.  It is completely okay to have personal preferences, we all do.  The danger is when that personal preference is placed on everyone else.  If it is a sin, it is wrong.  Period.  But, if it is YOUR personal conviction and you place judgment on someone else because they don't have that same conviction, Beloved, you are not honoring God, you're grieving His heart.

Question of the day:  Do you judge *sin* or do you judge people based on your personal preference?

Quote of the day: "It is the Holy Spirit's job to convict, God's job to judge and my job to love." Billy Graham

Prayer: Oh Father God, please forgive me for when I have judged others, not for the sin in their life, but because they did it differently than me. Forgive me for the times I have allowed my personal preferences to rule as a universal principle, making room for prideful judgements. I ask that You give me wisdom to discern when I do this and I ask that You make me exceptionally sensitive to this as well. I desire to honor You, not grieve Your heart because of my judgement. Set me free from the weight of judging those who are different than me. I know I can count on You to help me. Thank You Jesus and it's in Your strong Name I pray, Amen.


Further Scripture Reading:

Psalm 75:7

James 4:12

# Day 16

"When she heard about Jesus, she came up behind him in the crowed and touched his cloak, because she thought, "If I just touch his clothes, I will be healed." Mark 5:27-28

And guess what? She was. Healed from twelve long years of bleeding. Doctors had done who-knows-what to this woman but instead of getting better, she continued to get worse. Then, she heard that Jesus of Nazareth was walking through her town. It was crowded. Very crowded. There were many people bumping into each other and the Bible says that people were pressed in around Jesus. This woman reached out to touch Jesus' clothes because she knew the power that He held. Jesus asked, "Who touched me?" The crowd was pressed in around him and this woman was not the only one who had touched Jesus. The difference between all of those other touches and this woman's touch was the faith behind it. Jesus didn't scold her for touching Him or re-direct her to see the disciples first. He told her that her faith had healed her. The faith behind that touch is what healed her broken body. When this woman reached out in faith, Jesus received her. It's the same with you and I, Beloved. When we reach out to Jesus in faith, He receives us and makes us whole. Maybe you've been bleeding and wounded in your heart for years, just like this woman. Reach out to Jesus, trusting Him to heal your bleeding heart. He will stop the bleeding. He always does.

Question of the day: Have you ever felt like the woman in the story?

Quote of the day: "He touched me, Oh He touched me, and oh the joy that floods my soul! Something happened and now I know, He touched me and made me whole." Bill Gaither

Prayer: Abba, thank You that I can reach out to You in faith and You make me whole. Lord, my faith in You is strong and I believe that You can heal me from whatever is causing me pain. You bled so my bleeding would stop. Thank you for always receiving me and never turning me away.

I pray this all in the steadfast Name of Jesus, Amen.

Further Scripture Reading:

Mark 5:24-34

Worship: One Touch by Nicole C. Mullens

# Day 17

"Yet, O LORD, you are our Father. We are the clay, you are the potter; we are all the work of your hand." Isaiah 64:8

Throw. Glaze. Kiln. Centered. Pulling. These are some of the words that my friend, Jaclyn, uses on a daily basis. Her vocabulary is way cooler than mine. See, she's an artist, illustrator, and a potter. I know, I know, she's amazing! I really do have the greatest friends. Anyway, I watched a video she posted on Facebook about how she created a mug. It was the neatest thing to watch. I watched as she had to pound and pound the clay and then she put it on the potter's wheel. She moved her hands in a certain pattern, creating something amazing. Then it had to go into the fire. Once it came out it could be uniquely decorated and made into a one of a kind piece. Then, back in the kiln it went again. It made me think of this verse above. The Lord is the Potter, we are the clay. He uses His hands to form and fashion us. The clay must trust the Potter to create it into something useful, something beautiful. There is a process to it all. It doesn't happen quickly. Each step is necessary to turn the clay from a useless lump of earth into something meaningful and purposed. Jaclyn said, "The reason that I love pottery so much is because of the steps and what God spoke to me when I was learning this process." The Master Potter teaching His student, a fellow potter. How beautiful. Now, I'm not a potter but I am the clay and as clay, let me say that I choose to trust the Potter. I trust the process that I must go through in order to be what I've been called to be. I'm not thrilled when I have to go into the fire, not thrilled at all, but I know it's necessary. I don't know if I'm supposed to be a mug, a platter, or a spoon, I just know that whatever my Potter sets His hands to, I'm in. How about you?

Question of the day: Do you see the connection between the potter and the clay and The Potter and the clay (you)?

Quote of the day: "The clay needs the potter. We need God. We need Him because without Him we are nothing. But, when you are in His hand, you have potential, worth, hope, and promise. The

potter doesn't really need the clay but if the clay ever wants to be anything, it needs the potter."
Karen Mutchler Allen


Prayer: You are the Potter and I am the clay. I trust You to mold me into whatever it is You want me to be. I don't always like the process I have to go through because it involves fire but I know that I need the Master Potters hand. Help me to be moldable and pliable, not hardened or unusable. Thank You for the process that leads to the final product. You are a faithful Potter and I love you. I pray this in Jesus Name, Amen.


Further Scripture Reading:

Jeremiah 18:6

Romans 9:21


Worship: The Potter's Hand by Hillsong

# Day 18

"Wait for the LORD; be strong and take heart and wait for the LORD." Psalm 27:14

What does a McDonalds drive-thru, a microwave, a cheetah, and a jet all have in common? Yup, you guessed it…they are fast. Well…mostly fast…there's been a few McDonalds lines that were slower than a turtle chasing a sloth. Don't we just *love* things that are fast? We are a "fast-food", "hurry-up", "microwave" society. We want it done yesterday. Here's what I've noticed…we have taken that same mentality into our prayer life as well. We go to God with a need or a request and then want it answered in a millisecond. Can God do that? He sure can. Does He? Sometimes. But often we must wait for the answer. Here's the thing though, God doesn't ask us to wait because He wants to torture us, He asks us to wait because He sees it all. He sees what would happen if He answered that request right now. He sees how the wait will cause us to grow and depend on Him. He sees that there is something better waiting ahead instead. He sees it all. When He asks us to wait, He's asking us to trust Him. He's asking us to trust the future He has for us...the good future...the hope-filled future...the one we are waiting for. If you have asked Him for something and His answer to you is, "Not right now, just wait." then my challenge to you is this...wait. You don't even have to stop asking for it...just know that He will answer your longing and your heart's desire when He knows it's time. I understand the struggle...I'm in it right now. I've asked, and asked, and asked some more. It's been years and His answer remains the same...wait. Have I gotten discouraged in this waiting game? Yes, I have. Often, actually. But here's what I cling to...if God says wait then I will do so because I can trust Him...and so can you.

Question of the day: What is something you have prayed for and God's answer was "wait"?

Quote of the day: "If you've asked God for answers but find yourself waiting longer than you planned, take a moment now to thank Him in advance for His answer. Trust that He is working behind the scenes on your behalf. Don't give up. Look forward in hope and expectancy for Him to respond and remember that the Lord is good to those who seek Him." Leah DiPascal

Prayer: God, I confess that I often come to You with a request and want You to answer it immediately. I can get frustrated when Your answer is to wait. Help me to trust when You give me that answer knowing that You are working for my good. I trust You for it, I believe You for it, in Jesus Name, Amen.

Further Scripture Reading:

Lamentations 3:25

Micah 7:7

Worship: Take Courage by Kristin DiMarco

# Day 19

"By this everyone will know that you are my disciples, if you love one another." John 13:35

Have you ever had someone ask you to do a favor for them and not say "thank you" or "I appreciate you for helping me out?" Well...I did. Someone that I don't know all that well asked me for a favor. It wasn't convenient and would be out of my way to do so but I said, "Absolutely!" I did "it" and that person never said, "Thank you!" And are you ready for this...they never even recognized that I actually did it. Nothing. Nada Zilch. It made me mad. Frustrated me. Left me saying, "I will NEVER do anything for them again." Period. Done. I'm out. Then...I heard Him. He whispered to my heart. He spoke words of Truth over me. "This is what I call LOVE dear one. Doing something for someone and never expecting anything in return. Not recognition. Not a response. Not gratitude. Not anything. Not ANYTHING. Serve those who will never "deserve" it. Serve those who will never give you a word of thanks...and serve them often. Every time they ask. Every.time. Serve them. Love them. Be My hands and feet. Yes. This is love. This is what will stir Me to say on the day you stand before Me, "Well done my good and faithful servant. Thank you."

So....I will go against my flesh. That thing that hollers, "That's not fair!" or "That's just horrible manners!" I will stand tall against the feeling of being disrespected or unappreciated. I will choose to remove pride and think, "I deserve a thank you!" or "I DESERVE at least some recognition of my effort to serve that person". And instead, I will serve this person again. And again. Not because I FEEL like it. Not even because I WANT to. But because this is love. Love. LOVE. And they will know we are His because of it...

Question of the day: Have you ever had a situation where you had to love someone in this way and if so, was it easy?

Quote of the day: "Don't love to be loved in return. Love for the sake of loving." Connor Chalfant

Prayer: Dear Father, help me to love others the way You want me to…the way You'd love them. I want to serve and love them so much so that they ask me why! May love be my anthem, the song I sing so that others will know that Your love abounds in me. I ask that Your love flow through every part of me so I may love. Thank You for Your love Father! I ask all of this in Your Son's precious Name, Jesus, Amen.


Further Scripture Reading:

Mark 12:29-31

1 John 3:16-19

# Day 20

"But encourage one another daily, as long as it is called "Today," so that none of you may be hardened by sin's deceitfulness." Hebrews 3:13

If you've spent any time near water then you've seen a barnacle. Probably a lot of them. A barnacle is a type of crustacean that, as larvae, attaches itself (permanently) to anything it finds. They fix themselves like unwanted guests onto piers, buoys, rocks and of course, boats. These pesky and annoying arthropods aren't really a problem if you keep moving and regularly keep your boat maintained. However, leave your boat in the water sedentary for any length of time and you'll have a long hard job in front of you. Did you know that the US Navy spends millions every year on hull maintenance to remove barnacles? Did you also know that people can be barnacles? Not the kind that stick to the bottom of boats, but the kind that cling to people, seemingly annoying and pesky. People who are barnacles don't really add value to the other person. They just attach themselves and hitch a ride. Doesn't sound like a very beneficial relationship, does it? We should add value to those we are around. We should be encouragers. The word "encourage" means "to infuse courage". Do you infuse courage into the people you spend time with?  There was a man in the Bible named Joseph, a Levite from Cyprus, who the apostles called Barnabas.  Guess what Barnabas means?  It means "son of encouragement".  Did you notice that his real name was Joseph but the *apostles* saw something different in him and renamed him Barnabas.  A nickname of all nicknames!  This guy, Barnabas, infused courage into the people he spent time with.  He inspired.  He gave hope, confidence, and spurred others on to greater things.  It sounds like Barnabas spent no time mirroring the barnacles ability to cling to something, adding no value.  Barnacles have no purpose and only are seen as pesky, clingy parasites that weigh objects (or in this case, people) down.  Barnabas' purpose was to encourage.  To spur on.  To bring life to.  To infuse courage into.   If I had the choice to have either one of these visit me on a boat at the lake, I can tell you in a heartbeat which one I'd invite. I can assure you it wouldn't be the one I'd have to scrape off the bottom of my boat.


Question of the day:  Are you a Barnabas or a Barnacle?


Quote of the day:  "Everyone has the potential to become an encourager. You don't have to be rich.

You don't have to be a genius. You don't have to have it all together. All you have to do is care about people and initiate." John C. Maxwell

Prayer: Lord, I don't want to be a barnacle. I want to add value and encourage those around me. Help me to be a Barnabas and infuse courage into others. May I be the one who inspires and provides hope for those You bring into my path. Bring to my mind ways I can encourage others today! I believe You for it, I trust You for it, in Jesus Name Amen!

Further Scripture Reading:

1 Thessalonians 5:11

Hebrews 10:24~25

# Day 21

"Then those who feared the LORD talked with each other, and the LORD listened and heard. A scroll of remembrance was written in his presence concerning those who feared the LORD and honored his name." Malachi 3:16

One of the biggest lies I tell myself is, "I don't need to write *that* down, I'll remember *that*." I don't remember *that*. Ever. God doesn't need to write anything down because, well, He's God and doesn't have a 40-something year old memory. God writes things down so **we** can understand its importance. The Bible tells us that when we, His people, talk about Him, He listens and hears. Not only does He listen and hear but those moments are *written down* in His presence! When you share with a friend that God answered your prayer, God hears and makes a note. When you tell your children of how God protected you in a certain situation, it's written down. When your small group shares the goodness of God, it too is noticed. Don't be afraid to talk about the Lord. Don't hesitate to lift Him up in front of others. Don't be timid in sharing the wonders, works, and miracles He has done for you. Go ahead friend, talk about Him! Each time we as believers talk about the Lord, share His goodness, tell of His acts, or lift His Name to each other, God hears AND He writes it in a scroll of remembrance. Those precious conversations with other believers do not go unseen or unheard by the Creator of the Universe. So, keep talking, my friends, keep talking.

Question of the day: How often do you talk about the Lord with others? In the scroll of remembrance, how long would your list be?

Quote of the day: "You have never truly found Jesus if you do not tell others about Him!" Charles Spurgeon

Prayer: Father, help me to talk about You. Your faithfulness. Your greatness. Your provision. Your miracles. All of it Lord. Thank You for writing the moments I do talk about You down in order for me to see just how important it is to You! You are worthy to be in the middle of my conversations and You are worthy to be talked about! I want to lift Your Name up and make much of You Jesus! I pray that from today on, the list that is written under my name in Your scroll fills pages upon pages.  Thank You Lord!  I love You and praise You in Jesus Name, Amen.

Further Scripture Reading:

Psalm 96:2-4

Luke 8:39

Worship:  What a Beautiful Name by Hillsong

# Day 22

"The LORD is good to those who wait for him, to the soul who seeks him." Lamentations 3:25

I loathe waiting. Like REALLY loathe it. Not a big fan. I don't like waiting in line. Or for a parking spot. Or for my food. Or for my Amazon packages which is why I'm a Prime Member. Get the picture? I just don't like waiting. The Lord has found this to be an issue with me and is working on it and personally I don't find it funny…at all. Waiting is hard. There's the unknown, the tendency to want to be in control, and the fact that I am a microwave kind of girl asking to wait for the crockpot . But see, here's the thing, I've learned that when I wait for God to answer a prayer or deliver on a promise, it strengthens me and builds my courage as well as my faith. I've also learned that there's a REASON behind the waiting. In my walk with Him, I've had to wait for a lot of things and for many different reasons. Timing, growth, and protection are just a few of the reasons God asked me to wait. Sometimes I waited well. Other times I failed miserably. But what I can promise you, Beloved, is this...if He is asking you to wait, trust Him and just do it. He's worth waiting for.

Question of the day: What is God asking you to wait for and how will you wait?

Quote of the day: "Biblically, waiting is not just something we have to do until we get what we want. Waiting is part of the process of becoming what God wants us to be." John Ortberg

Prayer: Oh God, help me wait well. Whatever you are asking me to wait for I trust You with it. Waiting is hard but I want to be strong and take heart because You are good and You will deliver on Your promise. When I get impatient and want to move ahead of You, remind me that You see around every corner and if You haven't answered my prayer or given what You've promised there is a reason . I choose to wait for You because You have proven to be trustworthy. I love You and am thankful for how You love me back. I pray this in Jesus Name, Amen.

Further Scripture Reading:

Psalm 130:5-6

Isaiah 40:29-31


Worship:  While I'm Waiting by John Waller

# Day 23

"Plans fail for the lack of counsel, but with many advisers they succeed." Proverbs 15:22

What college should I attend? Who should I marry? Do I buy a house and if so, which one? Is this the best job for me or should I look for another? Decisions, decisions. Adulting is hard isn't it? So, what do you do when you have a hard decision to make? Do you heed Nike's slogan and just "Do it"? Do you take time to mull it over? Do you ask for advice? Some people think that asking for advice is a sign of weakness or that if you ask others for counsel it makes you unwise. I don't believe that. Did you know that The President of the United States has 10-12 advisors that he seeks counsel from? If he needs those 10-12 people to help him make wise decisions, doesn't it sound like a wise idea for us too? Tiger Woods, one of the most successful golfers in history, has a coach. He's someone that will help Tiger make decisions about the game that he plays and the career that has made him a millionaire. I have a feeling that Tiger is a better golfer than his coach but he sees the value of the coach's counsel. It's okay to know when you don't know. It's also okay to ask for wisdom when you need it. Are you in the midst of making a hard decision? Ask for counsel. Wise people don't pretend to know. Ask…it doesn't mean you lack wisdom, it's the evidence *of* wisdom.

Question of the day: Who can you ask for wisdom and counsel in your life when making hard decisions?

Quote of the day: "He that won't be counseled can't be helped." Benjamin Franklin

Prayer: Father God, help my head and my heart to know when to ask for wise counsel when I have to make hard decisions. Help me to know when I don't know and to ask for help from those You've placed in my life who can offer me wise counsel. I know I need direction and I also know that You will provide me with it through others. Thank You Lord! I love you and I pray this in Jesus mighty Name Amen.

Further Scripture Reading:

Proverbs 12:15

Proverbs 19:20-21

# Day 24

"Be very careful, then, how you live—not as unwise but as wise, making the most of every opportunity, because the days are evil." Ephesians 5:15-16

It's about time.  No, really, it's about *time*.  Life is all about time isn't it?  If we were to be honest, our time = our life, doesn't it?  Life, and time, pass quickly…too quickly if you ask me.  God cares how we spend our time.  See, the real question we should be asking is not, "What time is it?" but rather, "What are we doing with our time?"  Are we making the most of every opportunity we've been given?  Are we spending quality time with the people we love?  Are we investing time into our children?  Are we spending the necessary time getting to know God on a deeper level?  Time, if not managed well, will slip away.  It will evaporate.  We have to be intentional about how we spend our time.  I believe our priorities and our focus will aid in how we choose to invest our time.  Maybe you are crazy busy at work and really have just dropped the ball when it comes to spending necessary *quality* time with your wife and kids. Maybe the TV, Facebook, or your cell phone has captured your attention so much so that you barely look up when your kids talk to you. Maybe one of your hobbies like fishing, tennis, golfing, or shopping has taken the place of spending valuable time making memories with the people in your life. In the Greek, "making the most of every opportunity" is translated as "redeeming the time". It needs to be redeemed because it's a fleeting commodity. How are you redeeming the time in your life? Redeeming your time isn't always easy because you have to make an **effort** to do so. You must be intentional on how you spend your time....because it's tickin'. Your time and how you spend it matters to God and it should matter to you as well. It really is about time, isn't it?

Question of the day: What are some ways you are making the most of your time?

Quote of the day: "Time can be an ally or an enemy. What it becomes depends entirely upon you, your goals, and your determination to use every available minute." Zig Ziglar

Prayer: Lord, I recognize how important the time You have given me is and I am asking You to help me make the most of it. I need You to show me where I have let time slip away or have not been intentional with it. The time You have given me is precious and I confess that at times, I have not treated it as so. Please forgive me and know that I desire to redeem the time from today on. Help me today to look at my time as something to be invested in wisely. How I spend my time is important to You and it's important to me as well. Thank You for helping me Abba to see it that way. I love You and I pray this in Jesus Name, Amen.

Further Scripture Reading:

Psalm 90:12

Proverbs 27:1

# Day 25

"Without warning, a furious storm came up on the lake, so that the waves swept over the boat. But Jesus was sleeping. The disciples went and woke him, saying, "Lord, save us! We're going to drown!" Matthew 8:24-25

Storms can be scary. Really scary. You know that first hand if you've ever been in the middle of one. Storms can sometimes be seen coming miles away but sometimes they just come out of nowhere, wreaking havoc on everything in its path. Come to think of it, I've NEVER sat through a bad storm and thought, "Wow, this is just really nice. I LOVE sitting through this storm...it's just so... relaxing." It's stressful and laced with uncertainty and anxiety. Just like we can't escape the storms that the weather produces, we also can't escape the storms that *life* produces. The storms in life WILL happen, it's inevitable. But here are a few things to remember when faced with a storm in your life. First, remember that you are not alone. Just like Jesus was in the boat in the verses above, He's with you too. Now, you may be like, "Ummm....Karen, did you not see that Jesus was

ASLEEP in that boat?" Yes, I noticed that, but He woke up didn't He? I've often thought that I would like to have enough faith in Jesus during a storm to just let Him sleep. Jesus was there with them through that storm and He's with you too. Second, you can trust Jesus to help you through the storm. This is something you don't have to do alone. This storm is not one that you have to fight by yourself. You can trust Him in the storm. He's not afraid. He's not worried. He's not freaking out. The storm that surrounds you is still under His authority. Jesus knows how to handle storms, Beloved, He created the wind and the waves after all, didn't He? Life is often riddled with storms. Severe, threatening, harsh, fierce storms. I wish we didn't have to go through the hard stuff in life, but we do. You aren't alone in the boat and you can trust Jesus to handle the storm for you. He's not asleep. He's not taking a cat nap. He's reminding that storm that He's in charge of it all.

Question of the day: How does it make you feel knowing that Jesus is with you during the storms of life?

Quote of the day: "We all face storms in life. Some are more difficult than others, but we all go through trials and tribulation. That's why we have the gift of faith." Joyce Meyer

Prayer: Jesus, thank You for being with me in the middle of the storm and for helping me through the hard times in my life. I trust You, knowing that the winds and the wave must obey You. I ask that You continue to help me remember that storms may come, but You, You are in control and You are the anchor that holds. I love You and thank You in Jesus Name, Amen.

Further Scripture Reading:

Matthew 8:23-27

John 16:33

Worship: Eye of the Storm by Ryan Stevenson

# Day 26

"Then the mother of Zebedee's sons came to Jesus with her sons and, kneeling down, asked a favor of him. "What is it you want?" he asked. She said, "Grant that one of these two sons of mine may sit at your right and the other at your left in your kingdom." Matthew 20:20-21

This sounds just like a mama doesn't it? This mama walks right up to Jesus and asks Him to allow each of her two sons the privilege of sitting on either side of the King of Kings…no biggie. All I could think of when I read this was the phrase, "Jockeying for position" which means to maneuver or manipulate for one's own benefit. This expression, dating from about 1900, originally meant maneuvering a race horse into a better position for winning. That's what she was doing, maneuvering and manipulating so her boys could get the best seat in the house! The need to have a position, even spiritually, is quite common but God doesn't promote spiritual *position*. He promotes spiritual *direction*. There is a big difference. There is no hierarchy of believers. There is no "spiritual rank", placing one believer above or below another. WE do that, but God doesn't. This spiritual journey is not about "arriving" at a certain position, it's about growing in your spiritual maturity. Spiritual position says, "If I do this or that, I will be placed at a higher rank with how God sees me." Spiritual direction says, "I will strive to mature in my walk with Christ." There is no ranking or ladder in this journey. Stop trying to jockey for position next to Jesus…He's already beside you anyway…and leave the jockeying to the horses.

Question of the day: What do you think about spiritual position vs. spiritual direction?

Quote of the day: "God doesn't promote spiritual position, He promotes spiritual direction." Karen Mutchler Allen

Prayer: Lord, help me to grasp the truth that You don't have a hierarchy of believers or show favoritism with Your children. Your concern for me is in my spiritual direction and in my maturity as I learn to walk with You. Help me to shake off the need to "earn" a spot beside You and remember that You are already there by choice. Beside me. Help me to not jockey for position and realize that the only position I need to be in is bowed at Your feet. I pray this in the most precious and perfect Name of Jesus of Nazareth, Amen.

Further Scripture Reading:

Matthew 20:20-28

Acts 10:34-35

# Day 27

"The LORD is my shepherd, I shall not be in want." Psalm 23:1

Have you ever wondered why David called the Lord his "shepherd"? Well, David had been a shepherd his whole life. Even as a young boy, he fought for his sheep. He killed lions and bears when they threatened his flock. David watched over those sheep and cared for them with great diligence. David called the Lord his shepherd because he could relate, it was what he knew. David wasn't familiar with any other title to give the Lord so he gave Him the only one that meant something to *him*, "Shepherd". I've heard on many occasions that the Bible refers to us as sheep because sheep are dumb animals. Now, I've done some dumb stuff in my life…okay, REALLY dumb stuff, but I don't think that's how God sees us. I also don't think David was calling himself dumb. I think the example of sheep is used because there are not many other groups of animals that have a human as their leader on a consistent basis. Not to mention the trade of shepherding was one that was well known during Bible times. Sheep do better when they are led, and so do we. David saw how God cared for him and related it to how he cared for his own sheep. It was a beautiful and intimate connection he shared with his Lord. This ministered to my heart greatly and this revelation helped shape how I read Psalm 23. It's an earthly shepherd talking to his Heavenly One. It's a sheep trusting his Shepherd.

Question of the day: How is the Lord your shepherd?

Quote of the day: "Does the sheep need to know how to use a complicated sextant to calculate its coordinates? Does it need to be able to use a GPS to define its position? Does it have to have the expertise to create an app that will call for help? Does the sheep need endorsements by a sponsor before the Good Shepherd will come to the rescue? No. Certainly not! The sheep is worthy of divine rescue simply because it is loved by the Good Shepherd." Dieter F. Uchtdorf

Prayer: Lord, You ARE my Good Shepherd. You care for me, fight for me, search for me, and love me more deeply than I could ever imagine. It brings me peace knowing that You look after me like a shepherd would look after his flock. I mean more to you than any sheep because I am Your child. The LORD is my Shepherd, I shall not be in want. Thank You Abba. I love you and I pray this in Jesus Name, Amen.


Further Scripture Reading:

Psalm 23

# Day 28

"We were filled with laughter, and we sang for joy. And the other nations said, "What amazing things the LORD has done for them." Psalm 126:2-3

Boy do I love to laugh. And laugh. And laugh some more. Lots of things make me laugh too. One of my nieces and I can't help but to laugh when people fall down. We think that is just hilarious. (I won't mention her name but her initials are MLS) I laugh at those funny Memes on Facebook. I laugh at my own hilarious jokes. I even laugh at other people's laugh. My friend Jim has the BEST laugh in the history of the world. When he laughs at *anything*, I'm dead. I just can't get over how his laugh makes ME laugh! Did you know that laughter is actually GOOD for you? When you laugh, endorphins are released into the blood stream. These natural pain relievers promote a sense of relaxation and wellbeing. Deep belly laughter is also positively linked to the lymphatic and immune systems, helping those who laugh often have an increased immune system. When you laugh, your brain releases endorphins, interferon-gamma (IFN), and serotonin which are mood enhancers. These are only a few of the positive benefits to laughing. Listen, I've been in church my ENTIRE life so I know what you are thinking, "Girlllll, I've SEEN Christians…they walk around with their faces all serious and scrunched up like they've been sucking on lemons!" I know, I know, I've seen them too, but I'm here to tell you that it's okay to laugh, not *even* if we are Christians, but BECAUSE we are Christians! Don't take yourself, or this life, so seriously. Yes, there are times to be serious but there is also plenty of time to laugh…and laugh. Laughter is so good for you and I challenge you to laugh every day. Every.single.day. You may think that you won't have something to laugh at every day, well, if that's the case, just let me know. I'll give you Jim's number and HE'LL make you laugh!


Question of the day: What makes you belly laugh?


Quote of the day: "Laughter is poison to fear." George R.R. Martin

Prayer: Father, thank you for the gift of laughter! Thank you for knowing us so well that you gave us a way to express our joy, humor, and satisfaction. Remind me to laugh more, Lord. Sometimes I take this life and this world way to seriously and I often miss out on the joy that awaits me. I choose to laugh and laugh often, knowing you have given me so many things to laugh about. You are a joyful Abba and I'm thankful! I love You and I pray all of these things in Your precious and Holy Name, Jesus, Amen.


Further Scripture Reading:

Job 8:21

Proverbs 17:22

# Day 29

"For we live by believing and not by seeing."

2 Corinthians 5:7 (NLT)

I've always been a sucker for a good birthday party. Mine…yours…anyone's really. The birthday cake is always my favorite but a close second has to be the games. See, I love cake AND competitions. There's a litany of fun birthday games out there but the one that I always loved the most was "Pin the Tail on the Donkey". Remember that one? So, basically, there's this picture of a donkey's butt taped to the wall and your job was to stick the donkey's tail right in the middle of his rear. Sounds easy enough, right? Well, the game is made more difficult because they *blindfold* you and then *spin* you around a bunch of times and send you on your way. Whoever pins that tail the closest to where his actual tail *should* go, wins! I remember playing this game at a party when I was younger. They had just spun me around several times (which made me want to hurl the yummy cake I had just eaten) and said, "Go!" So I went. I took off in the

direction of that donkey's butt. I just KNEW I was
going to win (I told you I was a bit competitive).
Everyone was cheering and laughing and I was
excited to be announced the winner. Once I stuck
that tail on the wall, I took off my blindfold. Ya'll,
I wasn't even close. I had stuck that stupid
donkey's tail to the lady's kitchen cabinet. We
NEED to see, don't we? We NEED to know where
we are going. It just makes sense. Seeing is
believing, right? Well, actually believing is
believing. As a child of God, we are to walk by
faith not by sight. We are to believe what God
says instead of seeing what might come next. We
want to see the next step but God wants us to trust
Him. Faith, believing what you cannot see, is
difficult, I know. So how do you reconcile the fact
that YOU want to see but GOD wants you to trust?
Ask yourself these questions: Has God ever asked
me to do something that wasn't in my best
interest? Has God ever abandoned me? Has God
ever made a mess of my life? If you answered
"No" to any of these questions, then you need to
know that walking blindfolded with the King is
better than walking with eyes wide opened on
your own. God is faithful and trustworthy to lead
you without filling in all the blanks. We live and
walk by faith, believing that God will never let us

down.  See, Beloved, He's walking with us and beside us during it all…with Him, we'll never pin the tail to the kitchen cabinet again!

Question of the day:  Do you live by believing or by seeing?


Quote of the day:  "As you walk through the valley of the unknown, you will find the footprints of Jesus both in front of you and beside you."
Charles Stanley


Further Scripture Reading:

Hebrews 11

# Day 30

"But because my servant Caleb has a different spirit and follows me wholeheartedly, I will bring him into the land he went to, and his descendants will inherit it." Numbers 14:24

When I was in High School, I was definitely different then a lot of the people I went to school with and different wasn't always considered popular. I was known as a "goody-goody" and a "Jesus Freak". I certainly wasn't perfect but I knew that I wanted to pursue God's heart for me and if I was considered different, then so be it. I wasn't invited to a lot of parties in High School and the parties I *did* get invited to, I often left early...but I was okay with that. In fact, I preferred it that way. Being like everyone else was boring to me. Still is. (Have you seen my hair?) In a way, I could relate to Caleb. He had a different spirit about him and followed the Lord wholeheartedly. I don't regret being different or following Christ with my whole heart when I was younger because I am now an adult who does the same thing. It's okay to be different when it comes to following Christ. People will recognize it but even more importantly than that, GOD will recognize it, just like He did with Caleb. Different is good. Trust me.

Question of the day: Do you have a different spirit about you and follow Christ wholeheartedly?

Quote of the day: "Being different and thinking differently make a person unforgettable. History does not remember the forgettable. It honors the unique minority the majority cannot forget." Suzy Kassem

Prayer: Lord, thank you for singling out Caleb for being different and for how he was following you. Help me to focus on being different than everyone else when it comes to loving and serving you. May I do it wholeheartedly without my heart being divided. I love that you see different as good...help me to see it that way too. I love you and I pray this in Your good, good, Name, Amen.

Further Scripture Reading:

Daniel 1:8-16

Matthew 22:37

# Day 31

"The LORD appeared to us in the past, saying: "I have loved you with an everlasting love; I have drawn you with unfailing kindness." Jeremiah 31:3

"Our love is unconditional, we knew it from the start. I can see it in your eyes, you can feel it from my heart." I can still remember George Strait singing this song in the movie, "Pure Country". There he was, on stage, with his guitar and black cowboy hat, singing in that deep southern drawl about unconditional love. Swoon. Double swoon. Sorry guys, I know that is not *at all* what you want to read right now…but…I'm a chic, so…deal with it. George was singing about the very thing that we ALL long for (yes, even dudes!) Unconditional love. Love with no conditions. Unqualified, unlimited, unrestricted love. If you have ever been in a relationship where you have not received unconditional love, then you know just how big this is. Maybe you grew up with your parents putting conditions on their love. If you performed well, got good grades, were polite in front of others, made your bed, etc, then you were

shown love.  Maybe even lavished with love.  But, if you did not perform well, failed a test, weren't as polite, or didn't make your bed, love was withheld.  Maybe it was in a dating relationship or possibly even in a marriage.  What you did or didn't do, said or didn't say, determined how much love you were shown.  Regardless of the type of relationship, conditional love is debilitating, exhausting, and confusing.  So, what would you say to an "UNCONDITIONAL" kind of love?  I bet you think it doesn't exist, don't you?  You may think that there's no such thing but I'm here to tell you that there is, and it's wonderful!  God loves you with an everlasting love.  Check out the synonyms for everlasting:
eternal, endless, perpetual, undying, abiding, endu ring, infinite, boundless, timeless, and never-ending.  See, God loves you with a never-ending love.  A perpetual, abiding, and enduring love.  One that isn't determined by what you do or how you look.  It isn't given or withheld based on your performance.  One of my favorite pastors, Jason Britt, said something that was freeing and life-changing one Sunday.  He said, "There is nothing you can do to make God love you more.  And there is nothing you can do to make God love you less."  He just loves you.  Plain and simple.  There are no

strings attached. No caveats. No fine print. It's His love, given to you, forever. Maybe George Strait should write a song about that...I know I'd listen to it.

Question of the day: How does it feel to know that God has no conditions on His love for you?

Quote of the day: "Though our feelings come and go, God's love for us does not." C.S. Lewis

Prayer: Lord, unconditional love is so hard for me to grasp, especially when it comes to You. It's so hard for me to understand that I don't need to do anything to earn Your love. Oh God, help me know that You love me, period. You just *love* me. There is nothing I can do to make You love me more and there is nothing I can do to make You love me less. I want to believe that truth, God. Help me to walk like a child who is unconditionally loved by their Father. I trust You for it, I believe you for it, in Jesus Name, Amen.

Further Scripture Reading:

Deuteronomy 7:9

Romans 8:38-39

# Day 32

"There is a time for everything, and a season for every activity under the heavens" Ecclesiastes 3:1

I live in Georgia. Middle Georgia for that matter. It's hot, ya'll, like really hot. It's hot in the spring, the summer, *and* the fall. Come to think of it, the winter isn't all that cold either. Every year when I decorate for Christmas outside, I wear shorts. Shorts. I've always found it interesting that no matter what season we are in, we tend to complain about it and are ready for the next one. In January, we are ready for March. In March, we are ready for June. In June we are ready for October. Seasons are...well...for a season. There's an ebb and flow to the weather *and* to our lives. Could you imagine if it was winter all the time? Or if it not only rained in the month of April, but every single day of the year? What if this ninety-seven degree weather wasn't just from June to August, but it stayed through February? Seasons are a good thing! A season is not forever and if you've ever been in a tough season in your life, that is something to be thankful for, isn't it? I'd encourage you to embrace the season you're in, knowing that it will pass. It may pass like a kidney stone, but it *will* pass. Seasons also bring about change. We don't like change though, do we? But I think you'd agree that change is often necessary. Change can bring about growth so if you are in a season of change, know that it is creating in you something worthwhile, something deeper, and something worth allowing. I've also noticed that Seasons bring perspective. When I was in the season of wiping butts, noses, and anything else that could possibly leak on a tiny human, I'll be honest, I wanted that season to be OVER…quickly, I might add. Now, I'm in a different season of watching my kids drive away in an actual car and looking at what colleges they should apply to. In a crazy twist of ridiculousness, I find myself longing for those days of endless poop and pee. See, perspective. Whatever season you are in, be "all in" and know that this season will pass to another season…and be present in that one too. Try not to get so caught up in the next season that you miss the beauty of the one you are in. As far as seasons go here in Georgia, if you are looking for me from May until about October, you'll find me in my pool…I'll save you a float.

Question of the day:  Do you struggle with being present in the season of life you are in right now? Why or why not?

Quote of the day:  "We must remember there are different seasons in our lives and let <u>God</u> do what He wants to do in each of those seasons." Joyce Meyers

Prayer:  Thank You, Father, for the Seasons of Life. Help me to see those seasons in a positive light and help me to be present.  I don't want to wish my way to the next season because I just may miss something important that is waiting for me. Thank You for all the times You've seen me through a hard season in my life.  I find such hope in that and it helps me to carry on.  You are faithful in every season, Abba.  Thank You.  I pray this in the strong Name of Jesus, Amen.

Further Scripture Reading:

Daniel 2:21

Romans 8:28

# Day 33

"Blessed are those who mourn, for they will be comforted." Matthew 5:4

"Good grief Charlie Brown!" Sound familiar? Lucy from Peanuts was notorious for this phrase. I've always thought that was a weird statement...*good* grief? Is there such a thing? Grief comes from a loss. A loss of a loved one, a loss of job, a loss of a dream, etc. Loss can happen on many levels which in turn, causes grief. No one likes grief or having to grieve but if you live for even a minute in this world, you know that grief is inevitable. Have you noticed that everyone grieves differently? There are five stages of grief: denial, anger, bargaining, depression and acceptance. Not everyone goes through all five stages nor does everyone go through them in the same order. We are all made differently therefore, our grief will look different. You may be thinking, "Karen, this is not a very encouraging devotional today...geeze..." I know, this seems heavy, but grief is real...but so is Jesus. Do you know what the opposite of grief is? You may want to immediately answer, "JOY" right? I think that's a good answer but do you want to know what I think the opposite of grief is?  Hope.  Yes, hope. Not the kind of hope where you say "I hope it doesn't rain" or where you "hope you get the job" but real hope.  The hope that Jesus is real.  The hope that heaven is all that He says it is.  The hope that you are loved and cared for by the Creator of the world.  The hope that even though you are swallowed by grief, there is joy waiting for you. Hope.  It is a powerful motivator in the middle of grief.  Oh Beloved, I wish I could take the pain and grief away, but I cannot.  But what I can do is remind you of the hope that you have been given in Jesus.  He is your anchor.  He is your tomorrow. He is your song.  If you are grieving at this moment, please know that you are not alone. Jesus walks with you, dear one.  Grief can be deep, intrusive, and it can swallow you whole.  But there is hope in your grief and His Name is Jesus.


Question of the day:  In your grief, how has Jesus been your hope?


Quote of the day:  "But there is hope in your grief and His Name is Jesus."  Karen Mutchler Allen

Prayer: Oh Jesus, You are my hope in my grief. I know You see me and I am not alone. Help me to rest in You. Sorrow can be so overwhelming and I confess that without You, I am lost and drowning in a sea of grief. Show me what it looks like to walk in the hope that You have set before me. Hope that declares You have me securely in the palm of Your mighty hand and that I am safe and tended to. Jesus, I trust You with my grief and my sorrow because You are my hope. Oh how I love You Jesus. Thank You and I ask that You seal this within me by Your precious blood, Amen.

Further Scripture Reading:
Psalm 62:5

Hebrews 6:19

Worship: I have this Hope by Tenth Avenue North

# Day 34

"He said to them, "Go into all the world and preach the gospel to all creation." Mark 16:15

I have a confession to make. I don't want to be a missionary in Africa. Whew, there, I said it. I remember when I was younger hearing of how we needed to share the gospel with the world. My prayer always seemed to go down like this, "God, I will tell everyone about Jesus. I will go wherever You want me to go to tell others about You. Except Africa. Please don't make me go to Africa. In Jesus Name, Amen." I'm not really even sure why Africa freaked me out so, but it did. If I were to think a little more about it, I would probably deduce that it wasn't actually *Africa* that I had an issue with, it was the fact that I would have to go far away to tell others about Jesus. Guess what I've learned? I've learned that I am called to be a missionary EVERYWHERE. And by missionary I don't mean living in grass huts eating the local cuisine consisting of plantains, cassava and Fufu. If I take the "mission" out of missionary, it's easy to see that my mission in life is to share Jesus with others. There are a lot of ways to accomplish this mission too.  Do I stand in the streets yelling at everyone to get saved because their time is near and throw my Bible in their faces?  No, I don't. I've seen this done before and I honestly don't believe that it accomplished its purpose, unless, of course, the purpose was for people to walk on the other side of the street to avoid the yelling man.  I share Jesus all the time.  Sometimes I even use words.  We preach by how we live.  By how we love.  By how we treat others.  Preaching the gospel doesn't mean yelling...it often means serving.  People don't care how much you know until they know how much you care.  We "preach" the gospel by how we treat strangers, children, or anybody else that could never repay us in any way.  We preach the gospel with how we treat our waiter or waitress.  We share Jesus with others when we tell them stories of how good our God is.  In the time we spend preaching and sharing Jesus, we may have the beautiful opportunity to actually lead a soul to the saving knowledge of Jesus Christ.  I've had several of these opportunities.  To be the one who led them to Christ.  But you?  You may have been the one to preach Jesus to them with your actions.  Your kindness.  Your attention.  You may have been the one to care for them in the way that Jesus was magnified and I was the one who got to lead them in the sinners prayer. You don't have to be a preacher or an actual missionary to be the one who brings the Truth of Jesus to those around you. Live in such a way that the mission of the gospel speaks for itself. Just for the record, I'd go to Africa if He asked me...but I'm kind of glad He hasn't asked me yet...I don't even know what Fufu is...

Question of the day: How do <u>you</u> "preach" the gospel?

Quote of the day: "Preach the Gospel at all times. When necessary, use words." St. Francis of Assisi

Prayer: Father, I desire to share the gospel with others because I know the power and the salvation that comes with it. Help me to see my mission of living a life that would preach the gospel of Christ to all those I come in contact with. Show me ways to share Jesus with others. Help me to think outside the box when it comes to preaching Your message of love, hope, and salvation. Use me,

God, as a conduit for Your gospel. I trust You for it, I believe You for it, in Jesus Name, Amen.

Further Scripture Reading:

1 Corinthians 1:17~18

1 Corinthians 3:6~8

# Day 35

"Thereafter, Hagar used another name to refer to the LORD, who had spoken to her. She said, "You are the God who sees me." She also said, "Have I truly seen the One who sees me?" Genesis 16:13

There were children lined up in the cafeteria of a Catholic elementary school for lunch. At the head of the table there was a large pile of apples. Near the apples, a nun had posted a note that read, "Take only one, God is watching." Moving further along the lunch line, at the other end of the table, was a large pile of chocolate chip cookies. Near the cookies was another note written by one of the students. The note read, "Take all you want, God is watching the apples." Isn't it amazing that God could watch the apples AND the cookies *at the same time!* We sometimes forget that He's God and He sees it all. He sees you too. That is a powerful statement because often, we feel unseen. Invisible. Hidden. Unnoticed. Have you ever felt that way? Maybe you feel like if you were to disappear, no one would notice. Or maybe you feel like people look past you, or even through you. Being invisible is only great if you are playing hide and seek. It doesn't work in real life, does it? Hagar, the one mentioned in the verse above, was feeling the same way. Unseen, unnoticed, invisible. But then, she has this moment with the Lord and she realized that He *does* see her. He *does* notice her. She is not invisible. Not to the Most High. She renames God and calls Him a Name that no one had ever called Him before...El Roi. The God who sees. God had never taken His eyes off her. And He doesn't take His eyes of you either, Beloved. You are seen. You are known. You are loved. It's never an "either or" with God. He isn't either watching the apples OR the cookies. He sees it all...and that includes you.

Question of the day: Have you ever felt unseen or invisible?

Quote of the day: "Hagar's God is the One who numbers the hairs on our heads and who knows our circumstances, past, present, and future. When you pray to El Roi, you are praying to the one who knows everything about you." Ann Spangler

Prayer: Lord, I confess that at times I feel invisible and unseen. Thank you for reminding me today that YOU see me. I'm never out of your sight, not even for a minute. When I have the overwhelming feeling of being unseen, help me remember that I am not invisible to You. There isn't a second that goes by where You take Your eyes off of me. I am forever loved by You. Thank You Father. You are El Roi, the God who sees me. I declare this truth in Jesus Name, Amen.

Further Scripture Reading:

Genesis 16:1-13

Psalm 121:3, 5-8

# Day 36

"Am I now trying to win the approval of human beings, or of God? Or am I trying to please people? If I were still trying to please people, I would not be a servant of Christ." Galatians 1:10

Are you a people pleaser? Do you feel responsible for how others feel? Do you apologize often or have trouble saying no? Do people tell you that you act like those you are around or do you need other people's praises to feel good? These are all signs that deep down, you have the desire to please people. It's not that it's bad to be thinking of others, in fact, the Bible tells us we should think of others before ourselves. It's just that *pleasing* others is not the same as *helping* others. Trying to please others is exhausting and futile. While it may yield some satisfaction in the short term, pleasing people isn't sustainable. Why? Well, because people are flawed. Finicky. Selfish. One day you may be able to please that person but the next, you may not. One day that thing you do meets the need, the next day, it doesn't. Exhausting. I'd challenge you to focus on pleasing God instead. See, He doesn't change. Pleasing

Him isn't a crap shoot. Want to have your mind blown? You actually don't have to do anything to please God except exist. That's crazy talk, right? Nope. It's the truth. God does not have a to-do list with your name on it. God is infinitely pleased with you, not because of what you *do* but because of who you *are* – His child. I've heard it said that if God had a wallet, your picture would be in it. Why? Because He loves and values you as His own. There's no check-list or amount of specified duties that could ever change that. God IS pleased with you. You don't have to spend your energy trying to please any one person…the only One that matters is already pleased.

Question of the day: How do you please God?

Quote of the day: "Trying to please others before pleasing God is inverting the first and second great commandments." Lynn G. Robbins

Prayer: Father God, I need you to know that I want to please You more than I want to please any person. Sometimes I fall into that rut of wanting their approval and I need Your help in reminding me that they aren't the ones that matter…You matter. I also choose to remember that pleasing You isn't a matter of 'doing', it's so much easier than that. Pleasing You happens because I am Your child and You delight in me just because I've chosen You as my Father. When I get bogged down with checklists and thoughts of having to "do" things to please You, simply remind me of Who's I am. Thank You for loving me the way You do…I love You so. In Jesus Name, Amen.

Further Scripture Reading:
Psalm 149:4
1 Thessalonians 2:4

# Day 37

"For God speaks in one way, and in two, though man does not perceive it." Job 33:14

Have you ever heard something in a sermon that really spoke to your heart? You know, something that really made an impact and you could feel it settle on your soul? Then, later that day, a song comes on the radio with the same exact message? And then at lunch the next day, you're chatting with a friend who brings up the same topic. Isn't that when you begin thinking, "Okay God, I hear You, I hear You!" Those moments are called Holy Echoes. It's when God wants to reveal something to you or desires your full attention. He doesn't just whisper it once, He echoes. God has done that for me on many occasions and I'm so thankful for all those echoes. Why? Well, because I know it's Him. It's not a coincidence or by accident. It's my Abba, letting me know He has something to whisper to my heart. It's Him sharing something special He has just for me, His daughter. I'd encourage you to listen out for those Holy Echoes now that you know what they are. Make yourself aware of those sweet echoes He sends your way. A song you hear over and over again. A word that continues to show up consistently. A topic that constantly is presented to you. Ready your heart and your spiritual ears to hear and know that your Abba is speaking to you. These Holy Echoes may be directives. They may be for the purpose of showing you what direction you should go, what decision you should make, what job you should take, etc. But it also may just be the echo of, "I love you" whispered in many ways from a Daddy who adores you. The purpose of Holy Echoes is simply for you to know He wants to commune with you. It's an invitation. I encourage you to listen closely for those echoes from now on. They are happening...don't miss them.

Question of the day: Can you think of a time when God has sent you Holy Echoes?
Quote of the day: "And like an echo, God often uses the repetitive events and themes in daily life to get my attention and draw me closer to himself." Margaret Feinberg
Prayer: Lord, thank you for all of the Holy Echoes You've sent my way in the past and I ask that I will be sensitive to those You have waiting for me. It gives me confidence to know that You will whisper one thing in many ways so I know it's You. I love You, I pray this prayer in the strong Name of Jesus, Amen.

Further Scripture Reading:
Job 33:14~33

# Day 38

"Be kind to one another, tenderhearted, forgiving one another, as God in Christ forgave you."
Ephesians 4:32 (ESV)

I learned this verse when I was in the first grade and have never forgotten it…even when I wanted to. Why would I want to forget it? Well, because kindness is hard at times. Kindness is not a feeling, it's an action. Think about it. You don't "feel" kind, you "act" kind. Want to know what I find incredibly ironic? Christians should be **THE** kindest people on the planet…but often we are not. We are selfish and in a hurry. Maybe we feel entitled to receive kindness instead of giving it. I really don't know what our problem is but I'm fairly sure that Jesus is tired of it…and so am I. Jesus was the kindest person who ever lived. He did kind things. He showed a level of kindness on this earth that I know is difficult but not impossible. What made Jesus so kind? Well, first of all, He had the heart of His Father. By the way, so do we. But secondly, He was intentional and aware of those around Him. He SAW people, like, really SAW people. Not what they were wearing or what they were doing, but He saw the person, the heart, the soul…and then He was kind to them. Those same two qualities that Jesus had abide in us as well. We have the heart of our Father. When we asked Him to come and live in us, He traded our hard heart for a heart like His. We have the ability to see others the way God does, because through Jesus, we have His heart. We, too, can be intentional and aware of those around us. When we are intentional about SEEING those around us, we will also see their need and meet it with a loving act of kindness. There are a bazillion ways to be kind to those around us. Buying someone's lunch at Chic-Fil-a, mowing a neighbor's yard, sending a card in the mail, holding the door, letting someone in front of you in the car-rider line, bringing a meal to a widow. The list is endless, ya'll. I want to encourage you, dear one, to slow down today and SEE people. Really *see* them. Then, be kind to them, however God is showing you to do that. There is nothing this world needs more than an abundance of kindness and as believer, we should be at the head of the pack, practicing the art of kindness. We are never more like Jesus than when we show kindness to others, whether we think they deserve it or not. Be kind. It's never the wrong thing to do...

Question of the day: What are some practical ways that you can show kindness to others today?

Quote of the day: "No act of kindness, no matter how small, is ever wasted." Aesop

Prayer: Father, help me to SEE others the way You see them and show them the kindness that You would. I'm sorry for the times I was too selfish or too busy to be kind to someone who needed it. Help me to be intentional and aware of those around me in order to show kindness. Put people in my path today that I can show the same kindness Jesus would. I choose kindness, today, Lord. I love You and I ask this in Your precious Name, Jesus. Amen.

Further Scripture Reading:
Luke 10:25-37

# Day 39

"Give thanks in all circumstances; for this is God's will for you in Christ Jesus." 1 Thessalonians 5:18

I kind of wish it didn't say "in all circumstances". I wish it said, "in most circumstances" or "when it's easy" or even, "when things are good." But there it is, in black and white…"in all circumstances." All. Sighhhhh. I remember when the Lord was leading our family to move. We had lived in the same area forever and were well connected and very content. Then, God had to go and shake it up and ask us to move two hours away. I didn't want to go. What I WANTED to do was cross my arms, stomp my feet, and pout. I did not feel like giving thanks…at all. We packed our things and moved to a place where we didn't know a soul. I remember dropping my kids off at school the very first day and thinking, "No one knows them. No one knows me. What if they need help? What if I need help?" Again, I did not feel like giving thanks…at all. I was thankful for our new house. I was thankful for the fact my husband was in a new job that I knew he'd be amazing in. I was thankful for some things…just not in ALL things. Then I began to see some things happen. I began to see how my kids were growing in the Lord. I began to see how they were maturing. I began to see that I was stronger than I realized. I began to see how much closer my husband and I were becoming because we had to depend on each other more than ever. I began to see that the five of us were filling in the gaps like never before. We were growing. As individuals and as a family. When I realized what was happening, I began to give thanks. For the move. For the separation. For the hardship. For the growth. For the heartbreak. For all of it. In all of the circumstances. I give thanks.

Question of the day: Do you find it easy to give thanks in all circumstances? Why or why not?

Quote of the day: "No matter what our circumstances, we can find a reason to be thankful." Dr. David Jeremiah

Prayer: Lord, help me to see the value of being thankful in all circumstances. The easy, the hard, and everything in between. When I am thankful, it allows me to see Your hand in my situation. I choose to be thankful in all things. I need Your help when I forget and I ask that You would set my heart towards thankfulness. I trust You for it, I believe You for in, in Jesus Name, Amen.

Further Scripture Reading:
Psalm 7:17
Psalm 95:2

Worship: Grateful by Elevation Worship

# Day 40

"We do not want you to be uninformed, brothers and sisters, about the troubles we experienced in the province of Asia. We were under great pressure, far beyond our ability to endure, so that we despaired of life itself. Indeed, we felt we had received the sentence of death. But this happened that we might not rely on ourselves but on God, who raises the dead." 2 Corinthians 1:8-9

Have you ever heard the phrase, "God won't give you more than you can bear?" I have and it drives me absolutely batty. Want to know why? Because it's not in the Scripture, that's why! Seriously, it is nowhere to be found in the Bible. What I think may have happened is that people confused it with 1 Corinthians 10:13 where it says, "No temptation has overtaken you except what is common to mankind. And God is faithful; <u>he will not let you be tempted beyond what you can bear.</u>." This verse is talking about temptation, not heartache or heartbreak. When I hear people say that God won't give you more than you can bear, I think of the young couple who just had to bury their one month old baby. I think of the grandmother who was driving the car that killed her grandson. I think of the family whose young son was diagnosed with cancer and not long after his mom was diagnosed with cancer too. I think of my friend who lost both of her parents within eighteen months of each other and now feels like an orphan. I think of the young girl who was molested by her father for years and years and no one knew. I think of my friend who was shot, raped, and left for dead but thankfully survived. Do any of these stories sound like something a person can "bear"? None of these stories can be "handled". God isn't dishing out tragedies on the people who He thinks can carry them on their own. If we could handle things on our own, we wouldn't need God or His matchless strength, would we? We wouldn't need Him to demonstrate His power in our life because we would have it all together. There are moments in this life that will absolutely slaughter us. Demolish us. Slay us. We aren't *supposed* to be able to handle it. We are *supposed* to crawl in our Daddy's lap and let Him be strong for us and through us. We aren't supposed to bear it…because HE is our burden bearer. He is strong when we are weak…and that is wonderful news, isn't it?


Question of the day: What are your thoughts on the phrase, "God won't give you more than you can bear?"

Quote of the day: "God's strength in your weakness is His presence in your life." Andy Stanley

Prayer: Oh Father, how I need Your strength in my life! I am not capable or equipped to handle heavy burdens but I know that You are. May I be quick to bring them to You and not feel like I have to handle hardships on my own. You are my Abba and You do not pour troubles on me because You think I'm strong enough to handle them. Instead, You want me to crawl in Your lap and ask for Your strength to pour over me. I am not able to handle these things on my own and need Your help. I know that You will always be with me, infusing Your strength into my weakened soul. Thank You Abba. I love you and I pray this in the strong Name of Jesus of Nazareth. Amen.


Further Scripture Reading:

Psalm 28:7-8

2 Corinthians 12:9-11


Worship: Trading my Sorrow by Third Day

# Day 41

"So do not fear, for I am with you; do not be dismayed, for I am your God. I will strengthen you and help you; I will uphold you with my righteous right hand." Isaiah 41:10

Fear says you can't. Fear says you won't. Fear says you'll fail. Fear says you're not worth it. Fear says nothing will ever change. Fear says a lot of stuff. Fear is a liar. The problem with fear is that it pushes its way into the deep places of your mind, crawls up onto the throne of your heart, settles in and makes its home. Fear is an unwelcomed royal guest and it's time to de-throne him. Just for a second, think about some of your fears. What are you afraid of? List the top five things that absolutely freak you out. Rate them from highest to lowest. Take a look at that list. Now, read the following quote from Michel de Montaigne from five hundred years ago, "My life has been filled with terrible misfortune; most of which never happened." Hmmmm…never *happened*. Only **8 percent** of your worries are worth concerning yourself about. <u>Eight</u> percent. There are definitely things we should have a healthy fear of. Healthy fears are those that involve certain things in life that can cause harm to us, either emotionally or physically. For example, it is perfectly normal and healthy to be scared of fire or tornadoes. After all, this fear is what likely keeps us from getting too close to a fire or trying to get a better look at a tornado. But see, healthy fears aren't the fears that trip us up. It's the unhealthy, irrational fear that causes us to curl up in a fetal position while we're tucked in a corner somewhere, sucking our thumb. You don't have to let fear run your heart or your mind. He doesn't belong on the throne of your heart, God does. God is with you, always. When you begin to feel fear and it's not the healthy kind, tell God. He already knows you're afraid, it's more for you than Him. Tell Him you need His strength and His help and He will help you handle your fear. Listen, I'm not asking you to be FEARLESS, I'm just asking you to fear-LESS. Remember, fear is a liar. Start telling him the truth and kick him off the throne of your heart…he doesn't belong there.

Question of the day: Do you struggle with fear and if so, how does this devotional help?

Quote of the day: "Fear defeats more people than any other one thing in the world." Ralph Waldo Emerson

Prayer: God, I believe that fear is a liar and he has lied to me for way to long. When I feel fear begin to speak to my heart and mind, I choose to cry out to You. I know You are with me and will give me the help I need to hear the truth. Sometimes fear cripples me, overwhelms me, debilitates me, and I'm tired of it. You live on the throne of my heart, not fear. Thank You for speaking Your truth to me today. I trust You for it, I believe You for it, in Jesus powerful Name, Amen.

Further Scripture Reading:

Joshua 1:9

2 Timothy 1:7

Worship: Fear is a Liar by Zach Williams

# Day 42

"If a man has a hundred sheep and one of them gets lost, what will he do? Won't he leave the ninety-nine others in the wilderness and go to search for the one that is lost until he finds it?" Luke 15:4 (NLT)


If a shepherd has one hundred sheep and one of them wanders off, how many sheep does this shepherd have? It's a simple math question, isn't it? I bet you want to answer 99, right? Well, the answer is actually one hundred. The shepherd had one hundred sheep. "Waaaiiittt a minute, Karen, you are REALLY bad at math!" Well, you're not wrong but in this case I'm actually dead on. See, even though the shepherd had one hundred sheep and one of them decided to go AWOL, the shepherd still has ONE HUNDRED sheep. It didn't matter to the shepherd that the sheep had wandered off, it was still HIS sheep. See...he had one hundred sheep. Some may say it was unwise and reckless of the shepherd to leave the ninety-nine sheep just to chase the one who chose to wander away. They may argue that the one sheep who left would deserve whatever came its way and that the ninety-nine didn't deserved to be left alone. That one sheep should just get what he deserves for leaving. I get that. I understand, I really do, but what if that sheep were *you*? Wouldn't YOU want to be found? Wouldn't YOU want to be sought after, helped, and saved? See, the above thinking usually comes from the sheep that are already in the ninety-nine group...*not* lost, *not* wandering, *not* scared. But that one...that lone sheep that has found itself lost, it needs its shepherd to find him. And guess what, that shepherd would move heaven and hell to find that sheep....just like the Great Shepherd moved heaven and hell to find you. Jesus came to seek and to save those who are lost. Our Great Shepherd will leave the ninety-nine in order to find you every.single.time....because you are His and He desperately loves you. That shepherd had one hundred sheep...he would have NEVER settled for ninety-nine...never.

Question of the day: Why would the shepherd leave the ninety-nine just for the one?

Quote of the day: "God pursues us for the purpose of a redemptive relationship." Dr. Gary Fenton

Prayer: You are the Greatest Shepherd ever. Thank You for searching for me and pursuing me even when it was me who did the leaving. Thank You for never giving up on me or leaving me on my own. I'm humbled to know that You think I was worth it…leaving all the others…just to get me. Thank You Jesus. I love you! I pray this prayer in the Name of the Greatest Shepherd to have ever lived, Jesus. Amen.


Further Scripture Reading:

Luke 15:1-7


Worship: Reckless Love by Cory Asbury

# Day 43

"My dear brothers and sisters, take note of this: Everyone should be quick to listen, slow to speak and slow to become angry." James 1:19

Whenever I had a college professor say, "Take note", I pulled out my pen and did just that...made a note. Why? Because if that professor took the time to tell us specifically to take note, it was more than likely very important and would wind up on the test. I feel like James just put on the professor's hat here and did the same thing with this verse. "Take note, Karen, this is important and it WILL be on the test...of life." What is so important that I should be retrieving my pen and paper? It's the wise counsel to be quick to listen, slow to speak, and slow to become angry. I believe I've also heard it said this way, "God gave us **two** ears and **one** mouth for a reason. We should listen twice as much as we talk!" Good point. Dually noted. We all have conversations (sometimes intense conversations) that happen where we want to be "right" or "heard". We go into that conversation with the intention of being "right". The problem with that mentality is that it goes directly against what James was teaching here. We have adopted a saying in our house (whether we like it or not) and it goes like this, "Seek first to understand, then to be understood." This.is.hard. Super hard at times. To go into a conversation with the purpose of trying to understand the other person's perspective, hear their take, and listen to their side isn't easy but it is the right thing to do if you are really trying to get to the bottom of the issue. If you just want to go into the conversation to be heard and to be right, then you will destroy the relationship instead of strengthening it or restoring it. I recently had to walk this out in a few different instances and I'm so glad I sought first to understand THEN be understood. It changes things for the better. This doesn't mean you have to agree with what they are saying, it just means you had the wisdom to let them say it. When entering a tough conversation, be quick to listen, slow to speak, and slow to become angry. Take note…there will be a test.

Question of the day: How can, "Seek first to understand and then to be understood" help you when it comes to tough conversations?

Quote of the day: "No behavior on our part is more self-centered than the demand to speak and the refusal to listen." Robert E. Fisher

Prayer: Father, help me be quick to listen, slow to speak, and slow to become angry. Help me seek first to understand someone then to be understood. It goes against my flesh because I want to be heard. I want to be right. Help me to see that by doing what You are asking, I am putting my flesh aside and making the health of the relationship a priority. I will need Your help to do this so I ask this in Your strong Name, the Name of Jesus, Amen.

Further Scripture Reading:

Proverbs 17:28

Proverbs 18:2

# Day 44

"Therefore, my dear friends, flee from idolatry." 1 Corinthians 10:14

When I think of an idol, I'm not going to lie, my first thought always goes to Billy...you know, Billy Idol. But immediately after that, I imagine a golden statue of some weird looking image that looks kind of freaky, but in truth, an idol can be way more subtle than that. It may not be golden. It may not be a statue. But it is still something we worship. Idolatry is defined as an extreme admiration, love, or reverence for something or someone. How do we know if we have an idol in our life? Marc Alan Schelske asks these three questions:

1. Have you recently said, "If only I could have _____, everything would be OK?"

2. Have you felt in your heart a sense of desperation that you're sure would go away if only you were acknowledged or loved by _____.

3. Have you felt anxiety or fear around the possibility of losing _____?

If you said "yes" to any of those, and you had a clear sense of what to put in that blank, then you know something about your own idols. Right about now, you may be feeling weak or even embarrassed that you have an idol in your life. Don't. See, our hearts were MADE to worship. We were *wired* to worship. The problem is when our worship becomes imbalanced with something other than Jesus. Mr. Schelske says, "Your heart needs to worship every day. Actually, your heart WILL worship every day. You get to decide what your heart will worship." Idolatry is "making a good thing an ultimate thing". What do we do if we have indeed made a good thing an ultimate thing? Well, in the Old Testament, they would smash the idols. Break them. Shatter them. We need to do the same. Maybe not physically, but you do need to *smash* the idea that the idol can fill you. *Break* the habit of worshiping it. *Shatter* the belief that it will complete your life. There is no idol worth trading God for…not even Billy.

Question of the day: What idols do you have?

Quote of the day: "When anything in life is an absolute requirement for your happiness and self-worth, it is essentially an 'idol,' something you are actually worshiping. When such a thing is

132

threatened, your anger is absolute. Your anger is actually the way the idol keeps you in its service, in its chains." Tim Keller

Prayer: Lord, please forgive me for the idols in my life and I ask for Your help in smashing, breaking, and shattering them! I choose to worship You and You alone. You are the only thing I want my heart to chase, my head to trust, and my soul to believe in. I love You Abba and I pray this in Jesus Name, Amen.

Further Scripture Reading:

Exodus 20:3-6

Jonah 2:8

# Day 45

"People look at the outward appearance, but the LORD looks at the heart." 1 Samuel 16:7

I'll never forget Halloween growing up. We had a stash of costumes in the attic that had been handed down to us and each year we would rummage through the box to find a costume. I had two brothers and there was always a hot pursuit for the best costumes in that box…first come, first serve. One year I lost…I was the last to the costume box. I had to be one of the seven dwarfs…again. I can't even remember which dwarf it was but I do remember that it had a FULL MASK. It covered my entire head. It had two itty bitty eye holes and an eensy weensy nose hole. That mask was terrible. I couldn't see OR breathe. All night I was fidgeting with the mask. Pulling left, then right. Up, then down. I should have been enjoying my trick-or-treat experience instead of wrestling with Grumpy. Or Happy. Or Doc. Or whichever dwarf I was. Did you know that life can mimic what happened to me on Halloween? Think about it. We wear masks in order to cover up what is really going on in our lives. Masks are intended to show one thing while hiding another. But just like me, you'll fiddle with your mask because it doesn't really fit right…it doesn't *feel* right. The reason it doesn't feel right is because it's not the real you. You will walk around adjusting the mask so it's just right. Moving it to the left or right in order to cover any hint of you. You will quickly maneuver the mask when it gets bumped or jostled so no one will see past the mask and catch a glimpse of the real you. The problem is, just like I missed out on an exciting night that Halloween because the mask was hindering me, you are missing out of *life* because your mask is hindering you. Look, I get it. We all want to appear like we have it all together. We don't want people seeing our mess, our chaos, our disorder. Can I tell you something? It's okay. The mess. The chaos. The disorder. All of it. It's okay. Drop your mask. You're missing out on life because you can't see or breathe in that thing. God sees you…the real you…and loves you perfectly. It doesn't matter how others see you, Beloved. God is waaaayyyyy more interested in the real you than some mask you are hiding behind. Masks are for Halloween…and in my experience, even then they don't really fit. Ask

Dopey. Or Sleepy. I still can't remember which one...

Question of the day: Do you wear a mask and if so why?

Quote of the day: "Wearing a mask wears you out. Faking it is fatiguing. The most exhausting activity is pretending to be what you know you aren't."
Rick Warren

Prayer: Lord, I'm tired of wearing a mask. Help me to leave it behind with the knowledge that YOU love me...all of me...perfectly and unconditionally. I've grown accustom to my mask and it will be difficult to drop it because I'm afraid of what people may think about who I really am...what I'm really about...what really makes me tick. But, I will trust You in this. Show me how. Thank You, Jesus, and in Your Name I pray this, Amen.

Further Scripture Reading:

Jeremiah 12:3

Psalm 44:21

Worship: If we're Honest by Francesca Battistelli

# Day 46

"It's in Christ that we find out who we are and what we are living for. Long before we first heard of Christ and got our hopes up, He had His eye on us, had designs on us for glorious living, part of the overall purpose He is working out in everything and everyone." Ephesians 1:11 (MSG)

Several years ago, Pastor Rick Warren of Saddleback Church in Lake Forest, California, wrote this little book title, "The Purpose Driven Life", ever heard of it? It was no biggie...it just sold over **thirty million** copies in **five** years. See, no biggie. Over thirty million people bought this book. Why? What could this book hold that could possibly woo thirty million people to spend fifteen dollars to buy it? Good question. Purpose. It speaks of purpose. We ALL want to know our purpose. Why am I here? What should I be doing? What was I made for? Purpose is life altering. Lack of purpose is stifling. Show me someone who feels stuck with no hope of changing, someone with really high highs and low lows, someone who ignores their dreams because they are scared to move on, someone who constantly feels like there is something missing in their life and I will show you a person with no purpose. Some people think that your "life purpose" has to be grandiose or daring…it can be…but it can also be simple and safe. With purpose comes passion and drive. Purpose brings focus and focus brings clarity. What are you really good at? What fills you up after you do it? What would you miss if you couldn't do it anymore? What would you do if you would be paid a million dollars to do it? What would you do if you were paid zero dollars to do it? Are they the same? They are for me. That's a pretty good indication of what your purpose is. We only get to live on this earth for a short time. Don't waste what precious time you have here living with no purpose. If you don't know what your specific purpose is, it's time to ask God. He knows. He's the one who put it in you.


Question of the day: What is your purpose?

Quote of the day: "The two most important days in your life are the day you were born and the day you find out why." Mark Twain

Prayer: Father, I desire to live with purpose. Show me what my purpose is and help me walk in it with focus, power, and resolve. Help me to make a difference here on earth AND in heaven. I ask this in Your Name Jesus, Amen.

Further Scripture Reading:

Ephesians 2:10

1 Peter 3:9

# Day 47

"Yet it was because of this that God raised him up to the heights of heaven and gave him a name which is above every other name, that at the name of Jesus every knee shall bow in heaven and on earth and under the earth, and every tongue shall confess that Jesus Christ is Lord, to the glory of God the Father." Philippians 2:9-11

A few years back Lindsey and I went on a double date with some precious friends of ours to Athens. We ate at NOLA, which was one of our favs, and then went to play vintage video games at an arcade. (I promise we **are** adults) We headed home around 10:00 or so because we all had kids to put to bed and something happened that I will never forget. Ever. Our friend, Rob, was driving, Lindsey was in the passenger seat, and Crista and I were chatting in the backseat. All of a sudden we heard and felt something. I wasn't sure of what had happened and asked Lindsey, "What was that?" His response still echoes in my ears, "I think we just hit a person." My mind began whirling…a person, we hit an actual person, this can't be happening. Rob confirmed that we had indeed just hit someone. He called 911 and began to turn around to go back to the scene. Ya'll...I had no words. Me. The word girl. The girl with the gift of gab. Nothing. I had no words...except for one...Jesus. All I could do was cry out His Name over and over again. I could hear my friend Crista saying one word too...hers was Lord. So, like a rehearsed chorus, the backseat of this car was saying, "Lord Jesus, Lord Jesus!" It turns out that the man we hit was on drugs and the police had had dealings with him before. He was walking in the road at night and it was impossible for us to have seen him. He refused medical treatment but the officer said he would be hurting the next day....I can't even imagine. After it was all over, I couldn't help but think about our choices of words in that backseat. Lord. Jesus. Why? Why would those be the words that came from our mouths, but even more importantly, from our hearts? There are over 171,000 words in the English language and the only word that came to my mind was Jesus. Why? Because His Name is *Everything*. It's power. It's peace. It's healing. It's strength. It's hope. When words escaped me in a moment of pure terror, His Name is what I clung to. No long prayers or reciting verses. Just one Name. Jesus. There's just something about that Name, isn't there?

Questions of the day: What does the Name Jesus mean to you?

Quote of the day: "To holy people the very name of Jesus is a name to feed upon, a name to transport. His name can raise the dead and transfigure and beautify the living." John Henry Newman

Prayer: Jesus, Your Name is above all names. Your Name is the one I choose to call on when I'm in need. It's matchless. It's the Name we call on to be saved and it's also the Name we call on when we have no other words to say. Your Name is all we need. Thank You Jesus and in Your Name I pray, Amen.

Further Scripture Reading:

Matthew 1:21

Acts 4:12

Worship: Isn't the Name by Bethany Worship

# Day 48

"… being confident of this, that he who began a good work in you will carry it on to completion until the day of Christ Jesus.."
Philippians 1:6

When I was about 10 years old, I went to my first week-long camp experience…Camp Haluwasa. It was such a great week and it was full of all the "typical" camp stuff you'd expect. Cabins, lakes, snack shacks, old friends, new friends, learning Jesus stuff, and a few moments of home-sickness. Oh, and a lot of dirty, gross laundry. The kind that could have walked home by itself. I remember the chapel time in particular. All the campers would cram in the sanctuary and we would sing songs and listen to a message. We sang a song that has stuck with me for all these years and it was called, "He's still working on me". I just sang the title in my head. Here are some of the words.

> "He's still working on me
> To make me what I ought to be
> It took him just a week to make

the moon and the stars
The sun and the earth and Jupiter and Mars
How loving and patient He must be
'Cause He's still workin' on me

There really ought to be a sign upon my heart
Don't judge him yet, there's an unfinished part
But I'll be better just according to His plan
Fashioned by the Master's loving hands"

Do you know why I loved that song so much…well, besides its catchy tune? I loved that song because it gave me hope. Now, I may not have truly understood *then* what I was feeling was hope, but I certainly do now. Hope that God wasn't finished with me yet. Hope that God wasn't just going to throw His holy hands in the air and declare, "She's too hard. She's not worth my time. I'm done with her." Hope that it was actually okay not to be all the way "finished" just yet. The ten year old me recognized that…and so does the forty-something year old me. He's loving and patient to continue to work on all the things in me that are "unfinished". It's a process. A journey. I'm further in this process than I was when I started but I'm far from finished. He's still working on me, to make me what I ought to be…and I'm so very thankful.

Question of the day:  How do you feel knowing that God is not finished working on you yet?

Quote of the day:  "I am currently under construction.  Thank you for your patience." Pinterest

Prayer:  Father, first of all, thank You for starting a good work in me.  Secondly, thank You for promising You will complete it.  Thank You for Your patience and Your kindness as You help me refine the things in my life that need to be worked on.  Thank You for never, ever, giving up on me.  I love You!  In Jesus Name, Amen.

Further Scripture Reading:

Isaiah 30:18

Philippians 2:13

# Day 48

"He was despised and rejected by men; a man of sorrows, and acquainted with grief; and as one from whom men hide their faces he was despised, and we esteemed him not." Isaiah 53:3

Rejection. It's an equal opportunity destroyer. It can come in so many forms too, can't it? You can be rejected romantically. You can be rejected for a job. You can be rejected by a friend. You can be rejected socially. The list could go on. See, an equal opportunity destroyer. I have never been rejected and then thought to myself, "Self, that was fun, I can't wait to do **that** again!" I wish rejection wasn't a part of life, but it is. Did you know that Jesus was rejected? People rejected His teachings and called Him a blasphemer. They rejected His religion because it didn't look like any religion they had ever known. They tried to stone Him, throw Him down a cliff, riddle Him with accusations, and they wouldn't even accept Him in His very own hometown. Jesus' rejection reached all the way to the cross. With each of His limbs that were stretched across the wooden frame and with each nail that was hammered into place, rejection rang out with a loud vibrato. You would think the rejection of Jesus would have died with Him on the cross that day so many years ago, wouldn't you? Sadly, it still happens even today. Jesus stands at the door of our hearts and knocks. He wants so desperately to enter in and make His home there. Every day, people reject the truth of the Savior. They refuse His offer of eternal life spent with Him in Heaven. Jesus suffers the ultimate rejection when one of those He created throws their hand in His face and say, "No, not today." Beloved, the type of rejection we face is hard and at times, heartbreaking. But know this, rejecting Jesus' offer of salvation is one that will only bring you death…forever. If Jesus is pressing in on your heart today for salvation, say yes. You will never regret it. Not even for a second.

Question of the day: Is Jesus pressing in on your heart for salvation?

Quote of the day: "Jesus came to save us: let us not reject this marvelous gift!" Pope Francis

Prayer: Jesus, I choose to no longer reject You. I receive Your gift of salvation today. I know I am a sinner and that You died on the cross for my sin. I believe that You rose from the grave on the third day and that You live in Heaven with Your Father. I ask that You come into my heart to live forever. Thank You for saving me. I love You, in my Savior's Name, Jesus, Amen.


Further Scripture Reading:

Romans 10:9

Revelation 3:20

# Day 49

"...and to make it your ambition to lead a quiet life: You should mind your own business and work with your hands, just as we told you..."

1 Thessalonians 4:11


"Stay in your lane!" I heard one of my daughters say to the other. Daughter A said something out loud that Daughter B had told her in confidence and now Daughter B was saying in no certain terms, "Stay in your lane!" meaning, "Mind your own business!" If only we could all heed Daughter B's advice...to stay in our own lane. But we don't, do we? We like to get all up in other people's business. We like to think we know better. We like to think we're "helping". We like to think we know more about what *they* need than *they* do. WE need to stay in our lane. The more I think about this idea of staying in my own lane, the more I realize how spot on it is. First of all, if I'm driving in my car, I'm going somewhere right? I'm heading to a destination. If I don't stay in my own lane, it's going to take longer to get where I'm going because the quickest way to get from point A to point B is a straight line, right? When I concern myself with other people's business, I'm swerving from where I should be focused on heading. Second, if I don't stay in my lane while I'm driving and I move into someone else's lane, I become a distraction. I distract other drivers and could easily cause an accident. It's the same when I don't mind my business. I become a distraction to others and it could very easily cause more problems. If I'm not careful, one day I'll choose not to stay in my lane and find myself on a collision course with an eighteen wheeler! I don't know about you, but I'm choosing to heed Daughter B's advice and stay in my lane.

Question of the day: Is it easy or difficult for you to mind your own business?

Quote of the day: "Ninety percent of all human wisdom is the ability to mind your own business." Robert A. Heinlein

Prayer: Father, help me to mind my own business. Give me the strength and the self-control to focus on the things that are in my life, not in the life of others. Remind me every time I begin to dive into someone else's affairs that I have plenty of things to do and to work on in my own life. Thank You for helping me stay in my lane! I ask this in the capable Name of Jesus, Amen.

Further Scripture Reading:

Proverbs 26:15

1 Timothy 5:13

# Day 50

"But as for you, be strong and do not give up, for your work will be rewarded." 2 Chronicles 15:7

"There are all kinds of courage," said Dumbledore, smiling. "It takes a great deal of bravery to stand up to our enemies, but just as much to stand up to our friends." This quote is from J.K. Rowling's book, <u>Harry Potter and the Sorcerer's Stone</u>. Ever heard of it? J.K. Rowling is now one of the most well-known authors in the world because of her work in the Harry Potter series. I bet you already know that movies have been made about the books and now Universal Studios has a theme park completely dedicated to all things "Harry". But what I bet you *didn't* know is that J.K Rowling had a rough ride to the top. Just three years before the first Harry Potter book was published, she had just suffered through a divorce, was on government aid, went through depression and was struggling to provide for her baby. She received twelve rejection letters for <u>Harry Potter and the Sorcerer's Stone</u>. Twelve. Finally a small London publisher gave her a shot but told her she couldn't use her name because boys wouldn't read a novel that a woman had written. It would have been fairly easy for J.K. Rowling to give up. Throw in the towel. Hear the fat lady singing. Quit. But she didn't. She just kept going, one foot in front of the other. Maybe you can relate. Maybe you are about a second away from quitting. Let me encourage you Beloved, don't quit. Don't give up. Please. I don't doubt that this situation, journey, or circumstance, is overwhelmingly difficult. I also wouldn't dare say that you just need to try harder or do better. But what I will say is that quitting isn't the answer. Not today. Press in and press on, my friend. Don't throw in the towel, use it instead to wipe the dirt off your face and keep moving forward. Quitting isn't how you will get where you are going. Don't quit. Harry Potter would say the same thing…only he would say it in Parseltongue.

Question of the Day: Have you ever felt like giving up or quitting and if so, how did you keep going?

Quote of the Day:  "Never, never, never give up."

Winston Churchill


Prayer:  Lord, I'm tired, frustrated, and I feel like giving up.  I really want to quit.  I need Your strength and Your courage to keep on going.  Help me to finish.  Help me to put one foot in front of the other and keep moving forward.  You did not put the spirit of a quitter in me…You said I was MORE than a conqueror.  I believe You will see me through.  I trust You, in Jesus Name, Amen.


Further Scripture Reading:

Galatians 6:9

James 1:12

# Day 51

"Let your light so shine before men, that they may see your good works, and glorify your Father which is in heaven." Matthew 5:16

Several years ago at Hebron Baptist Church's College and Career Ministry, I met a beautiful friend named Theresa. Not long after that, she met and married her prince, Jeff Little. Their life was full of love, laughter, and family. Just a couple of years ago, Jeff was diagnosed with cancer and began the fight of his life. Theresa and Jeff would always update us on their latest doctor visit or any new treatments on Facebook Live with "Live with the Littles". There is no telling how many thousands of people watched and followed this family as they walked out their faith. I loved watching those videos. Jeff would always make me laugh but it was their faith, their unwavering faith, that inspired me. Even when Jeff was in the middle of his battle, he would go and speak to the youth at Hebron, challenging them to walk out their faith in Jesus. He and Theresa both were constantly sharing, loving, and encouraging others in their own walk with Christ. He believed that God was real and told everyone so. On September 4th, 2018, Jeff got to experience of the most remarkable things a person could ever hope for…He got to see Jesus. Face to face. Jeff is now healed and made whole. During the celebration of his life, one of the pastors asked those in attendance, "If Jeff has made a significant spiritual impact in your life, would you raise your hand?" A sea of lifted hands extended heavenward throughout the entire sanctuary. So.many.hands. So.many.souls. Jeff's life, albeit as short as it was, impacted so many people. He made them better. His life spurred something deeper in them. That is what we are supposed to be doing here…entering people's lives in order to make an impact…here and in heaven. Jeff's life made a mark here on earth as he walked out his faith until it was made sight. Countless lives are changed because of one faith-filled soul. It made me wonder how many hands would be lifted if the pastor asked that same question on my behalf…

Question of the day: Is your faith making a difference in the lives of people around you?

Quote of the day: "When we get to the end of our life, the question playing over and over in our mind will be, "Did my life make a difference?" Brian Fleming

Prayer: Lord, may my life be used by You to make a difference. Show me what matters and then help make it matter to me. Help me live a life that spurs people on in their walk with You. Nothing else matters. Nothing. Thank You for helping me in the strong Name of Jesus, Amen.

Further Scripture Reading:

Matthew 5:13-16

Hebrews 10:24-25

# Day 52

"Then I heard the voice of the Lord saying, "Whom shall I send? And who will go for us?" And I said, "Here am I. Send me!" Isaiah 6:8

In elementary school, recess was the highlight of my day! Oh, who am I kidding, it was the same way for me when I was a teacher too! I LOVED recess and I LOVED all the games we'd play. One of my favorite games to play was kickball! I was good…but I was also a girl and girls never got to be captain. Not only that, but most girls didn't get picked first either. I vividly remember the two "boy" captains standing there, staring at their prospects, seemingly not impressed. Guess what they were staring at? A whole bunch of elementary kids raising their hands, jumping up and down and yelling, "PICK ME, PICK ME!" This was what Isaiah was doing in this verse. He was telling the Lord, "Pick me, use me, I'll go!" except it wasn't for a game of kickball, it was for God's Kingdom. I can remember several years ago I was spending time with the Lord. It was well before I began writing or speaking. I was pouring out my heart before the Lord and I could see a picture form in my mind. It was of a sea of people sitting down, criss-cross applesauce (I told you I used to be a teacher!). I knew in my spirit that they were all believers. There they were, sitting, not doing anything. I couldn't resist the feeling, the urge, the pull, to stand up. So I did. I stood up, raised my hand high in the air, and shouted, "Pick ME God! Use ME! I don't want to sit…please, God, pick me!" 2 Chronicles 16:9 says, "For the eyes of the LORD range throughout the earth to strengthen those whose hearts are fully committed to him." I felt like as the Lord's eyes were searching the earth at that moment, He searched the sea of believers who were all sitting down in the spiritual realm and His gaze stopped on me…because I was standing, hand in the air, asking to be picked, pleading with Him to be used. There have been so many times throughout the years when I will have finished speaking at a conference or written the last word of a book He gave me, and I'll think, "Why Lord? Why do You let me do this?" His answer pours over me like fresh water, "Because you stood up that day…you stood up."

Question of the day: Have you ever "stood up" and raised your hand to the Lord and said, "Pick me!"? Why or why not?

Quote of the day: "You do not have to be special, but you have to be available." Winkie Pratney

Prayer: Father God, today I choose to stand up in the supernatural where others are sitting down. I throw my hand high in the air and I say, "Pick ME God, pick ME!" I want You to use me for Your Kingdom because I'm tired of sitting. Let Your eyes stop on me today…I'm standing…use me, I'll go. Thank You Lord and I ask this in Your Son's precious Name, Jesus, Amen.

Further Scripture Reading:

Isaiah 6:1-8

# Day 53

"Do not grieve, for the joy of the LORD is your strength." Nehemiah 8:10

When I was little and in Sunday School, we would sing this song called, "I've got the joy!" Here's how it goes:

> I've got the joy, joy, joy, joy down in my heart
> Where?
> Down in my heart!
> Where?
> Down in my heart!
> I've got the joy, joy, joy, joy down in my heart
> Down in my heart to stay

Do you remember this one? Well, I LOVED singing this song and sang it *all* the time. There was only one problem...I sang it wrong. See, I thought the lyrics were: I've got the joy, joy, joy, joy down in my heart, down in my heart **TUESDAY.** "Tuesday" and "**to stay**" sounded very similar to me. So, oddly enough I thought I could only have joy down in my heart on Tuesdays. Not Mondays, Wednesdays, or any other days. Just Tuesdays. Imagine my complete relief when I found out that I can have joy in my heart **EVERY DAY!** Now, hear me, dear one, having joy every day of the week does NOT mean you have to be happy, giddy, or sing songs with the little bluebirds every single day. Happiness and joy are *similar* but not completely alike. I think joy is one step deeper than happiness. Happiness comes from the "happenings" around us. If things are going well, we experience happiness. Joy travels deeper. Joy is not dependent on your circumstances or what is happening around you. To me, joy is directly related to your belief in who God is in your life. It is a fruit of the Holy Spirit working *in* you. I can't really say that joy is a feeling that I feel, it's more of a state that my spirit lives in. Circumstances in my life affect my happiness but they don't have the ability to move my joy. Joy is steadfast because it is rooted in the strength of God Himself. That's why Nehemiah 8:10 uses both "joy" and "strength" to convey this truth. I can be unhappy about a circumstance or situation but still walk in joy. Sounds crazy doesn't it? Joy, *His* joy, walks hand in hand with His strength and will carry you through it all. Happiness is wonderful and I'm so very thankful that we can experience happiness. After all, a life without happiness would be bleak, dull, and sad. But joy? Well, the joy that comes with knowing who God is in my life and that He is my strength, is enough to make me want to sing that song every day…and twice on **TUESDAYS**!

Question of the day: Is the joy of the Lord your strength?

Quote of the day: "Joy is distinctly a Christian word and a Christian thing. It is the reverse of happiness. Happiness is the result of what happens of an agreeable sort. Joy has its springs deep down inside. And that spring never runs dry, no matter what happens. Only Jesus gives that joy. He had joy, singing its music within, even under the shadow of the cross." S.D. Gordon

Prayer: Father, I desire for Your joy to be my strength. I want the deep, constant, abiding joy that comes with knowing who You are. May it bring me strength when I walk through hard times, times where happiness fades, but Your joy carries me with strength. I'm thankful for all of the happiness You've allowed to bless my life but it is the joy I long for. Fill me with Your joy, Lord, I ask this in the powerful Name of Jesus of Nazareth, Amen.

Further Scripture Reading:
Psalm 16:11
Romans 15:13

# Day 54

"The LORD is my shepherd, I lack nothing. He makes me lie down in green pastures, he leads me beside quiet waters, he refreshes my soul." Psalm 23:1-3

Have you ever had an unexpected surgery or an extended illness? I have and it sure is tough. Not just physically, but emotionally and spiritually as well. I thought I'd just bounce right back from my surgery and shook off the warning from my doctors at the recovery time. Pride cometh before a "very long time laying in the bed". I know it's supposed to be "Pride cometh before a fall" but see, I would have had to actually get out of the bed in order to fall and I wasn't allowed to get out of the bed…so…yeah. Guess what? Sometimes God **makes** us lie down in green pastures. I have always found the word choice in this verse amusing. It doesn't say that God will *ask* us to lie down or even *suggest* that we lie down…it says that He <u>makes</u> us lie down. He makes us because He knows we won't do it ourselves. Did you notice *where* God makes us lie down? In green pastures. Doesn't that sound beautiful? And restful? And peaceful? It does to me. Why does God *make* us lie down in green pastures? I think He makes us lie down for a few reasons. First, He can see our need for rest when we cannot. We will run ourselves crazy, going and doing, and deplete ourselves of any overflow. We become tired, run down, and empty. But God, knowing us as He does, says, "Nope. No more. You are going to lie down and rest." I also think He makes us lie down when we need to hear from Him but we've been too busy to stop and listen. When you physically cannot get out of bed, walk around, or do what it is you normally do, you are forced to sit…and listen…and listen some more. Another reason I believe He makes us lie down is because from that position, we have a different perspective, don't we? When you lie down, the world looks different than when you are standing up. When He makes us lie down, He is helping us see things through a different lens or an alternate perspective. But God isn't doing any of this to punish you. He's doing this because He loves you. The Great Shepherd wants what is best for His sheep. So, the next time you find yourself with a lot of unexpected time on your hands, say to yourself, "Self, my Shepherd is making me lie down in green pastures. Okay God, I'll do it. Thanks for knowing me better than I know myself." Now, go lie down and take a nap before He **makes** you.

Question of the day: Has God ever made you lie down in green pastures? If so, why do you think He did?

Quote of the day: "Green means growth and I had always felt I had to be up and moving in order to be growing. Once I was "made" to lie down, I learned that having the opportunity to stop and ponder and pray and ask for understanding, were my green pastures of growth." Darla Isackson

Prayer: Thank You for being such a Great Shepherd and knowing what I need even when I don't. I don't like to be still or to rest but I know that there is great wisdom in doing so. Thank You for the times You have made me lie down in green pastures. I love You and thank You, in Jesus Name, Amen.

Further Scripture Reading:
Matthew 11:28-30
Hebrews 4:9-11

# Day 55

"Get rid of all bitterness, rage and anger, brawling and slander, along with every form of malice."
Ephesians 4:31

Let's talk football, ya'll! I know, I know, I'm a girl and I'm not supposed to know much about football, but I do. Football in the south is something special. I've heard it said that the South has four seasons: Winter, Spring, Summer, and Football. If you think about it, football can teach us a lot about life. In football, you live ten yards at a time. You are one of eleven players trying to move that pigskin ten yards. Sounds simple right? Ten little yards and ten other people to help you get there. Well, there's a bit more to it. See, there are eleven people on the opposite team that are doing their darndest to stop you. They will hit you, knock you down, and pile on top of you just so you don't make any headway. Sounds a little tougher, doesn't it? There's one more preverbal monkey wrench to be thrown into it all and it has to do with a little yellow flag. These yellow flags are the bain of any football lover's existence. The refs throw them when there has been a rule broken or an infraction by one of the teams. Let's say someone from the defense just blocked in the back or maybe the quarterback couldn't read the play called so there was a delay of game. These penalties cause you to lose yards and go *backwards*. Penalties are so frustrating because they are self-inflicted. The other team didn't do it to you...you did it to yourself. Think about how frustrating it is to watch your favorite running back break a tackle and run 46 yards for a touchdown only for it to be called back because one of his teammates got a penalty for a face mask. Bitterness, rage, anger, brawling, slander, and malice all act as yellow penalty flags. As you work to move forward in life, when you participate in any of those listed, a flag is thrown. Those are self-inflicted penalties in the game of life...your life. The Bible is very clear about what to do...get rid of them. If you have bitterness about a situation or a person in your life, you need to deal with it. Don't give it permission to bury itself deep in your heart and become a bitter root. Do you struggle with rage and anger? Do you struggle with constantly wanting to fight or maybe it's the things that come out of your mouth? Is that what's tripping you up? Look, get rid of it. Any of it. All of it. Those things are sabotaging your ability to make it those next ten yards. Getting rid of all of those yellow flags in your life will make the next ten yards a lot easier to conquer. You'll have a lot more first and tens, that's for sure. Oh, and go Dawgs!

Question of the day: Do you struggle with any of the "yellow flags" mentioned? What will you do about it?

Quote of the day: "We didn't tackle well today but we made up for it by not blocking." John McKay, Coach for Tampa Bay Buccaneers

Prayer: Lord, I confess my struggle at times with bitterness, rage, anger, fighting, slander, and malice. They are yellow flags in my life that are sabotaging my walk with You. I choose to get rid of them today, Lord. Help me as I trade them for forgiveness, peace, unity, encouraging words, and goodness. I believe You for it, I trust You for it, in Jesus Name, Amen.

Further Scripture Reading:

Ephesians 4:26-32

# Day 56

"Accept one another, then, just as Christ accepted you, in order to bring praise to God." Romans 15:7

Imagine sitting with your extended family at Christmas dinner. The fine china has been set out and all of the delicious food has been placed right in the center just waiting to be devoured. The blessing has been said and just as everyone begins to pass the serving dishes around, Uncle Carl says, "Can you believe those idiotic democrats? You can't be a Christian AND a democrat!" Now, envision a pastor's wife making this statement, "I really don't want her in my small group...I heard she had two abortions when she was younger." Or how about a mom who tells her teenage son that he can't be friends with a guy at school because he's gay? What about a banker who decides not to eat with a fellow colleague because the banker is a Christian and the colleague is a Muslim? Ya'll, we've got this whole "accepting" thing wrong. So wrong. This verse tells us to accept one another, just as Christ accepted you. What Christ did when He accepted us, even when we were sinners, was love us...in spite of our choices. I'm not sure where we got the idea that if we accepted someone who lived differently than us, we are saying that we agree with *every* choice that they have ever made. No one does that.

When my husband chose to marry me, he chose to love and accept me even though he may not have agreed with every decision I have ever made in my life, sin or not. You could easily change out the word "accept" for "love". "*Love* one another, then, just as Christ *loved* you, in order to bring praise to God." Our love for others is found in our acceptance of them and not our agreement with the choices they may or may not make. It's quite possible to be in a relationship with someone and not agree on all decisions. Jesus did this very thing on many occasions, one of them being when Jesus defended a woman caught in adultery, but didn't condone an inappropriate relationship (Jn. 8:2-11). He loved and accepted her without agreeing with her choice. I have friends who are gay. I have friends who have committed adultery. I have friends who have had abortions. I have friends who have lied. I choose to love and accept them. Why? Well, the second part of the verse explains it…in order to bring praise to God. Jesus tells us to love God and love others. He never specified that the "others" are only the people who are exactly like us. Love relies on acceptance, not agreement. I am to love and accept others even if they live differently or choose differently than I do…that's what Jesus did for me. It's what He did for you too.

Question of the day: Do you love and accept others who choose to live differently than you?

171

Quote of the day: "The way we love the people we don't agree with, is the best evidence that the tomb is really empty." Bob Goff

Prayer: Oh Father, help me to accept those who live differently than me or make different decisions than I would make. Help me to love them like You do. Remind me that just because I love and accept them does not mean that I agree with all of their decisions. I often feel like I need to judge them instead of accepting them. Give me the supernatural strength to love them the way You would. Accepting them is what You choose to do, just like You chose to accept me and I am full of sin. I need You, Jesus. I ask this in Your mighty and worthy Name, Jesus, Amen.

Further Scripture Reading:
Romans 14:10-19

# Day 57

"If we are thrown into the blazing furnace, the God we serve is able to deliver us from it, and he will deliver us from Your Majesty's hand. But even if he does not, we want you to know, Your Majesty, that we will not serve your gods or worship the image of gold you have set up."
Daniel 3:17-18

So, I had every intention of writing this devotional about the blazing furnace that this verse was talking about and how we walk through fires in our lives. Every intention. But then, something happened. And that "something" was verse seventeen and eighteen. I couldn't get past it. To quickly sum up the story, there were three Jews (Shadrach, Meshach, and Abendego) who worked for King Nebuchadnezzar. This king had constructed a ginormous idol and commanded everyone to bow to it. These Jewish men refused and it sent that king into a tizzy. He told them in no uncertain terms that if they didn't bow, they would get thrown into a blazing furnace. The response from these guys just blows my face right off (pun intended). They basically said, "Our God is able to save and deliver us from this fiery furnace." Now, ya'll, this next part is what just slayed me. Then they said, "But even if he does not..." What the what? These men were telling the king that they KNEW God was capable of

173

saving them and that they KNEW God would rescue them from this trouble but *even if He didn't*, they would still serve Him. This stirred something deep within me. What would happen if I looked at the hard situations in my life with that same perspective? I know God CAN and that He is ABLE and even that He WILL…but even if *He does not*, I will serve Him. Oh, Beloved, don't You see? It is okay to BELIEVE that God will do something big in your life. It's perfectly okay to EXPECT that God will show up in your situation. It's completely appropriate to ANTICPATE that God will answer in the way you are asking. But to be able to say with all certainty, conviction, and trust, "But even if He doesn't…" Wow. Just wow. What trust, what confidence, what belief that phrase shouts. Even if He doesn't, He's worthy. Even if He doesn't, He's holy. Even if He doesn't, He's good. Even if He doesn't, He loves me. Even if He doesn't, He's enough. Even if He doesn't.

Question of the day: What does the phrase, "but even if He doesn't…" mean to you?

Quote of the day: "But even if He does not. That is slowly where God is moving me and how I long to respond as I face every giant crisis: knowing He is able to do all, but even if He does not, my faith will not waiver. We can't answer all the whys. We can't possibly grasp what His "good" is. But we

can choose to be steadfast, even if we don't get what we want. Our circumstances don't change His character and the truth about who He is."
Emily Roberts


Prayer: Oh my King...help my heart grasp this perspective. I know You *can* and I know You *will,* but even if You don't, I trust You. I believe that You are good. I settle in to the fact that sometimes You may not answer the way I think You should or how I want You too. Bring me to the place where I can honestly say "but even if He does not..." It speaks of my deep trust in who I believe You to be. I love You. But even if You don't...I trust You. In Jesus Name I pray, Amen.


Further Scripture Reading:

Daniel 3


Worship: Even If by MercyMe

# Day 58

"He has made everything beautiful in its time. He has also set eternity in the human heart..."
Ecclesiastes 3:11

There's this real tug-of-war that happens in my heart on some days. I long to go home. Not my geographical home but my home-home. Heaven. Now, don't go getting worried that I might end my life or anything. This is a longing that lives in my heart because God put it there. See, we weren't made for this world. We are passing through. The Bible even refers to us as "strangers" and "aliens"...not the kind that came out of Sigourney Weaver's stomach though...a totally different kind of alien, thankfully. I've often asked the Lord, "Why do I feel this tug? Why do I have this longing in my heart to go home to You?" His answer is in the Scripture above. He put it there. He has set eternity (or heaven) in the human heart. We BELONG there, with Him. When I feel that urge or tug it's because my spirit wants to go where it knows it belongs. Now, I don't want to be so heavenly minded that I'm no earthly good, know what I mean? I still LIVE here and while I am here, I am to make much of the Name of Jesus until I am called home. But I must tell you, this tug in my heart is what carries me through this life sometimes. I *am* a stranger. I *am* an alien. I *don't* belong here forever. And neither do you. We were made for me. Much more. So, I just want to take this time to tell you that when you hear that I have died, don't be upset (well, you can be a little upset, just sayin.). Just remind yourself, "Ahhhhh...she finally got to go *home.*"

Question of the day: Have you ever felt that tug?

Quote of the day: "If I find in myself desires which nothing in this world can satisfy, the only logical explanation is that I was made for another world." C.S. Lewis

Prayer: Father God, you created my heart to want to be with You in heaven forever. Thank You for loving me enough to set eternity in my heart. I long for the beauty of heaven and the precious opportunity to be in Your presence forever. While I am here on earth, sustain me and help me make much of Your Name. I love You, Abba. In Jesus Name I pray, Amen.

Further Scripture Reading:

1 Peter 2:11-12

John 17:13-19

# Day 59

"But You, O Lord, are a God merciful and gracious, slow to anger and abundant in lovingkindness and truth." Psalm 86:15

John Ralston, a football coach whose tenure spanned across more than thirty years, was quoted as saying, "I quit coaching because of illness and fatigue. The fans were sick and tired of me." Have you ever gotten to the point in your life where you thought the same thing? Not of football fans, but of God? Maybe you've said to yourself, "God is going to get sick and tired of me messing up." Or maybe you find yourself thinking, "I'm one mistake away from God leaving me this way." First, let me settle your heart a bit, God is not as fickle as football fans! Secondly, I understand your thought process, I really do. See, people in general have little patience for mess-ups, repeated mistakes, and errors. People are quick to wipe their hands clean of you if you prove to be a repeat offender in the world of uh-oh's. We all tend to work under the "three strikes and you're out" rule, don't we? Well, the good news is, God doesn't care about that rule. He's patient with us. He's merciful and full of grace. He doesn't grow weary of us being human. We *will* mess up, more times than we can count or want to admit, but we don't serve a God who is keeping track of our errors. He's not looking at a chart of our mistakes and saying, "Well, he only has one more mistake left and then I'm finished with him!" No, Beloved, His lovingkindness toward us is overflowing and abundant. There's no ticking clock to His grace. There's no countdown to when His mercy stops. I'll admit, I don't get it. I don't get how He doesn't just throw up His holy hands and quit on me. I'd quit on me if I were Him. I'd be sick and tired of my same old issues and hang-ups. I would want to throw in the towel and proclaim, "She's messed up one too many times for me…I'm out!" But not our Abba…nope, not Him. He doesn't grow sick and tired of us. He can't. He won't. His love won't allow it.

Question of the day: Have you ever felt like God was sick and tired of you messing up?

Quote of the day: "God never gives up on us—but tragically, all too often we give up on God!" Billy Graham

Prayer: Lord, I can't thank You enough for not giving up on me! Thank You for being merciful, gracious, and forgiving. Please help me to remember that You will NEVER give up on me and remind me to not give up on YOU! You know I'm human and You know I will make mistakes but I'm so humbled by how You treat me through it all. I'm so thankful, Lord. I pray this in Jesus Name, Amen!

Further Scripture Reading:
Joel 2:13
2 Peter 3:9

# Day 60

"As the ark of the LORD was entering the City of David, Michal daughter of Saul watched from a window. And when she saw King David leaping and dancing before the LORD, she despised him in her heart." 2 Samuel 6:16

When I was in college, God was doing something super big in my heart. I couldn't really explain it but I knew He was working deep in my heart and in my soul. This deep work of God seemed to always show up while I was worshiping….in the way of uncontrollable tears. Every time I would go to worship Him, I would just cry. Not loud, obnoxious sobs, just tears, steadily streaming down my face…and I couldn't stop them. One evening I went to a Bible study in a home and my friend led worship. Once again, the damn broke, and everything He was doing in me came out as liquid, pouring down my cheeks. I didn't sing a word. Not.a.single.word. I couldn't. I didn't even make a sound. After the Bible Study, a woman came up to me and said, "Why do you worship like that? All you do is cry. It's so distracting. Looks to me like you just want attention." I can't tell you how critically wounded those words left me. At this season of my life, my worship consisted of tears…tears for the work He was doing in me…tears for the thankfulness in my heart for how good He was to me…tears instead of words or songs. Later that evening, my friend asked what had happened. I told him and he reminded me of this story of David and his wife, Michal. David was so overwhelmed that the presence of God was coming to his city in the form of the Ark of the Covenant that David danced in his linen ephod. What is a linen ephod you may ask? Well, it's the equivalent to our "tighty whities". Yup, David was dancing in his drawers! While David was dancing before the Lord in praise and worship, his wife, Michal was in her tower, looking out her window, watching the whole thing unfold. When she saw her husband dancing in his underwear, the Bible says that she despised him in her heart. She looked down on him, and not just because she was in a tower. She made a judgement about the way he worshiped God. That is what the woman did to me that day. She judged my worship. Maybe because I made her uncomfortable. Maybe because she didn't understand it. Maybe because she was jealous of it. I really don't know why she judged me that day, but she sat in her tower and despised my worship to my King. The last verse of this chapter tells us that Michal had no children to the day of her death. She was barren. I believe that when we judge someone else's worship, we become spiritually barren. God won't bless any new birth in us. Why? Because worship to Him is holy and it's solely His…and He doesn't need our help determining who is worshiping the "right" or "wrong" way. I'd be lying if I said I've never looked down from my tower and judged someone's worship because I have. When I would see someone sitting in a worship service, arms folded, mouth shut, with no expression on their face, I'd think, "HOW CAN THEY NOT BE WORSHIPING THE KING?" Barren. I had to climb down from that tower and ask for forgiveness. Whether you think someone is worshiping "too much" or "not enough", those are both judgements unfit for us to make. *Worship as unto the Lord*…whatever that may look like…tighty whities and all.

Question of the day: Have you ever been judged for the way you worship? Have you ever judged someone else's worship?

Quote of the day: "The worship to which we are called in our renewed state is far too important to be left to personal preferences, to whims, or to marketing strategies. It is the pleasing of God that is at the heart of worship. Therefore, our worship must be informed at every point by the Word of God as we seek God's own instructions for worship that is pleasing to Him." R.C. Sproul

Prayer: Oh Lord, You are worthy to be praised! Father, forgive me for any judgements I've made over another person's worship. Please restore to me anything I've rendered barren because of those judgements. Worship belongs to You and You only. I'm so thankful I have the opportunity to worship You! I love You and praise You, in Jesus Holy Name, Amen.

Further Scripture Reading:
2 Samuel 6

# Day 61

"Don't be afraid of them. Remember the Lord, who is great and awesome, and fight for your families, your sons and your daughters, your wives and your homes." Nehemiah 4:14

I don't know if you're aware or not, but we are in the middle of World War III. Yup, smack dab in the middle of it. Don't tell me you haven't noticed? It's impossible to be alive right now and miss this war. It's the war on our families. An all-out assault on the foundation of family. It's not a new war, it's been happening since the beginning of time. See, satan started with the "parents" in the Garden of Eden. Adam and Eve were targeted by satan and when they listened to that slimy serpent, the first battle of many was won by the enemy. Satan didn't stop there, though. He immediately went after the "children" in the family as well. Cain and Abel. Satan won there too. Satan views families as a threat to his plans and has set his aims on destroying it at all costs. Nehemiah was experiencing this epic battle too. He wanted to rebuild the walls of Jerusalem that had been previously destroyed. Many of the surrounding enemies didn't like that idea and had devised a plan to attack all of those working on the wall. Nehemiah wisely had each man make repairs to the wall in front of his own house. Now there's some motivation to be sure you did a great job building the wall since it's in front of YOUR OWN house, huh?  As they continued building the wall, the enemies continued to press in and Nehemiah had had enough.  He called his people to fight for their families and then equipped them with weapons to do so.  In Nehemiah 4:17 (The Message) it says, "The common laborers held a tool in one hand and a spear in the other."  Those men were working at protecting their family with a tool in one hand and fighting for their family with spear in the other.  We all must do the same thing.  Building the walls of protection, healthy boundaries, and stability in our families as well as fighting for them…for their hearts, their minds, and their growth.  This is not an easy task but it is worth doing and doing well.  Satan is after our family.  He doesn't play fair and he has set his sights on the four people closest to me, my husband and my three kids.  What will I do, you may ask?  Well, I'll do what Nehemiah's people did.  If you need me, I'll be standing in front of my house with a hammer in one hand and a spear in the other.

Question of the day:  What are some ways that you protect and fight for your family?

Quote of the day: "There is no doubt that it is around the family and the home that all the greatest virtues, the most dominating virtues of human, are created, strengthened and maintained." Winston S. Churchill

Prayer: Father, our families are under attack and we need Your help desperately. Show me how to build with one hand and fight with the other. My family is worth protecting and fighting for. Guide me on how to do this well, Lord. I am trusting You with this in Jesus Name, Amen.

Further Scripture Reading:

Nehemiah 4

# Day 62

"Because he himself suffered when he was tempted, he is able to help those who are being tempted." Hebrews 2:18

I can walk by rows and rows of candy and not even bat an eye. Ike and Mikes, Sweet Tarts, Blow Pops, Starburst, you name it. I can pass right by homemade fudge or candy apples with no problem. Won't even give them a second glance. But if there is a yellow butter cake with vanilla butter cream within a five mile radius, I'll find it…and eat it. Cakes and pies are my jam. They tempt me. They call out to me in the middle of the night…or at breakfast…sometimes both. I have actually finished off the last HUGE piece of cake at 10:00 at night just so I won't be tempted to eat it the next day. Logical, right? Temptation happens to all of us. You may not be tempted to eat a whole cake like I am, but I can guarantee that there is something that temps you. Maybe it's porn. Maybe it's lying to your boss. Maybe it's gambling . Perhaps you're tempted to cheat on your spouse. Temptation is like a cruise ship…that eventually sinks. It promises to be a kickin' party but eventually the party ends. Did you know that *temptation* is not a sin? Nope. Now, what you do with that temptation is up to you. A temptation is a <u>desire</u> to do something, especially something wrong or unwise. See there…it's a desire…the *act* is completely up to you! Just because we are tempted to do something, doesn't mean we have to do it. Jesus was tempted by Satan himself. Satan is the author of all temptation, by the way. Jesus never fell into those temptations but it was clear that He suffered through the testing of it all. The Bible says that He was tempted in every way but did not sin. If Jesus was tempted in every way, then the temptations that face you are not foreign to Him. He can understand. He can relate. He suffered through it too. He is able to help you through this temptation…and the next…and the next. Ask Him, call on Him, rely on Him to help you. Remember, temptation in itself is not a sin. Choosing to delight in that temptation? Well, now *that's* a sin. I'm going to have to remember this the next time I see cake. Dang it.

Question of the day: If you were to answer honestly, what are your biggest temptations?

Quote of the day: "If we do not abide in prayer, we will abide in temptation. Let this be one aspect of our daily intercession: "God, preserve my soul, and keep my heart and all its ways so that I will not be entangled." When this is true in our lives, a passing temptation will not overcome us. We will remain free while others lie in bondage." John Owen

Prayer: Lord, temptation is pressing in around me and I feel its chase. Jesus, You have experienced every temptation known to man and I trust that You will help me when I call out to You. Remind me that I don't need to succumb to this temptation. I choose to overcome, to flee, and to walk away from whatever is vying for my attention that would not please You. I choose to lean on You, Jesus, and I ask this in Your powerful Name, Amen.

Further Scripture Reading:

1 Corinthians 10:13

James 1:13-14

# Day 63

"The nations will see your righteousness, and all kings your glory; you will be called by a new name that the mouth of the LORD will bestow."
Isaiah 62:2

Happy NEW year! I've got a NEW job! We bought a NEW house! That word "NEW" is redemptive isn't it? It's fresh, clean, and speaks loudly of hope. Would you like this to be a NEW year? How about a NEW day? So new that it smells squeaky clean? So new that the tags are still on? How about a NEW name? Not like an actual name, but one that doesn't carry every heavy moment over from the last year. You may have some names waving over your head like a banner. Names that have defined your journey thus far. Names that feel like a millstone wrapped around your neck, weighing you down. Names like, "Divorced", "Broken", "Depressed", "Single", "Damaged", "Unemployed", "Second-best", "Useless", and so many more. These words, these banners, fly over your head in the morning when you get up, wave over your head during the day, and then remind you of its position as you go to sleep. Well, the

Lord desires to give you a new name today. He will bestow it Himself because He is the ultimate Name-Giver. He wants a new banner to wave over your head. A new declaration of who you are and who you will become. Will you let Him?

Question of the day: What is the banner that has been waving over your head and what NEW name is God giving you?

Quote of the day: "With the new day comes new strength and new thoughts." Eleanor Roosevelt


Prayer: Father, I'm asking you for a new name. One that speaks of how You see me and what You want for me. The old banner has no place anymore. It has waved over my head long enough. As You give me my new name, may it settle as deep in my heart as it waves high above my head. It is for me to see but it is for others as well. May they be encouraged by the new name and the new banner that You have placed over me. May I walk this journey well, embracing the new, all the while thanking you for the ability to do so. Thank you. I love you. I pray this in Your powerful Name, Amen.

Further Scripture Reading:

Isaiah 43:18-20

2 Corinthians 5:17

# Day 64

"…he is a shield to those who walk in integrity, guarding the paths of justice and watching over the way of his saints." Proverbs 2:8

Picture a young mom with three small kids and a buggy full of groceries leaving Walmart. Just as this brave (and exhausted) mama gets to the car and begins to unload the children first, then all the groceries, she realizes that there is a pack of chewing gum in her purse. This is the same pack of chewing gum that she had put in her purse with the intention of buying it but didn't want the children to see it and begin fighting over who gets the first piece…or a whole piece…or the wrapper…or the…well, you get the picture. The dilemma ensues. She's in a pickle. She knows that she didn't pay for the gum and it would be stealing if she kept it. She also knows that she would have to get all three children out of their car seats, haul them back into the store, stand in line again, and purchase the gum. The thought that ran through my mind….I mean "her" mind was, "Seriously? Walmart will never miss this pack of gum and my kids will never know that I didn't pay for it. The easiest thing to do is just get in the car and go home." So, what would *you* do? Well, obviously I was this young, brave, and exhausted mom and I will tell you what I did. I got all three kids out of the car seat and hauled them right back into the store. I explained to the two oldest what had happened and that I would be stealing if I didn't come back to pay for the gum. We stood in line and waited. And waited. And waited. I began re-thinking my plan. We finally got to the cashier and I explained what happened. Guess what she said to me? She said, "You seriously brought this all the way back to pay for it? I would have just kept it, it's a pack of gum…no one would have ever known." My kids, who were now over **every single part** of grocery shopping, looked up at me like, "Mom…*she* even said it was okay!" I paid for the gum, walked back to the car, loaded the kids up and headed home. There were no balloons for my "good deed". There was no celebration for me bringing the gum back. No one threw me a parade because I did the right thing. But I knew HE knew and that was enough for me. Integrity has always been defined to me as doing the right thing even if no one is watching. Integrity is born of a person's character. It must be embedded deeply into a person's soul because after all, who's really going to take the extra time and effort to do the right thing when no one would ever *know* or *see* it was the right thing?  To me, integrity has nothing to do with <u>anyone</u> <u>else</u> but has everything to do with me and Him.  He sees.  He knows.  He's there.  If we were honest, integrity is not one of the hottest "character" commodities around, is it?  Why?  Well, I think it's because we don't really feel like we have much to gain by doing the right thing when we wouldn't get "credit" for it anyway.  There doesn't feel like there is a strong "end game" because there's no reward, no glory.  Proverbs 2:8 tells us a different story.  This verse tells us that when we walk in integrity, God is our **shield**, our **guard**, and our **watchman**.  That, Beloved, is worth its weight in gum.

Question of the day:  Do you walk in integrity?

Quote of the day:  "The things you do when no one's looking are the things that define you."  Anonymous

Prayer: Lord, I desire to be one who walks in integrity. I want to do the right thing, the hard thing, even if no one ever knows. YOU will know and that matters more to me than anything. Thank You for the promise to be my shield, my guard, and my watchman, as I walk this lonely road of integrity. May I always choose it, God. I love You, Lord, and I'm so thankful I can come to You and ask this in Jesus Name, Amen.

Further Scripture Reading:

Proverbs 10:9

Proverbs 20:7

# Day 65

"On hearing this, Jesus said to them, "It is not the healthy who need a doctor, but the sick. I have not come to call the righteous, but sinners." Mark 2:17

The coughing.  The sneezing.  The runny noses. The vomiting.  Ya'll...I LOATHE waiting rooms at the doctor's office.  I always feel like I'm going to catch something I didn't originally go in there with, know what I mean?  Like I came in for a sinus infection but I walk out with the pukey bug. Or I came in with a migraine but I walk out with pink eye?  No Bueno.  As much as I dislike waiting rooms, I am so thankful for doctors.  Doctors help sick people feel better, don't they?  But could you imagine overhearing this conversation in the doctor's office?

Doctor:  Okay, so what are you here for today?

Patient:  Well, I feel really great!

Doctor:  Ummmm...okay...so are you sick?  Do you feel bad?

Patient:  Nope, I feel like a million bucks!

Doctor: Well, I'm happy for you...but...why are you here? This IS a doctor's office, you know?

Patient: I'm perfectly healthy but I just thought I'd stop in!

Doctor: Alrighty...I have to go and see **sick** patients now but have a great day!

That doctor would be shaking his head and so would you after hearing that conversation, right? It doesn't make sense. Why would a healthy person need to see a doctor? *Sick* people need the doctor. This was the example Jesus used when talking to some very "churchy" folks. They had their spiritual panties in a wad because Jesus was eating with "sinners". Jesus reminded them that He did not come for the righteous people...they already knew Jesus. The righteous people already knew the truth. They already knew what it was like to walk in the healing Jesus offered...they weren't sick anymore. But the sinners...they needed a Savior. They needed to know the remedy. They needed to know the cure to their sickness. How can the sinners know if no one tells them? How can they know if no one ever spends time with them? Ya'll...how can we reach sinners if we always spend time with the saints? How can we share the truth with sinners if we never share a meal?  How can I ever lead a sinner to Jesus if I'm never around one?  Take a look at your life. Are you only ever around Christians?  When do you have the opportunity to be in the midst of those who are lost?  You can't seek to save that which is lost if you are never around anyone who *is* lost.  Sometimes as believers, we choose to wrap ourselves up in the church but forget why the church exists.  Jesus ate with the sinners.  Jesus spent time with those who weren't saved.  Jesus took the time to get to know those who didn't know Him.  All because He knew they were sick and He was the cure.

Question of the day:  In your daily life, are you around those who need Jesus?  If so, do you spend time building a relationship with them in order to share Jesus?

Quote of the day: "The naysayers of the day, the religious aristocracy, criticized Jesus as a "glutton and a drunkard, a friend of tax collectors and sinners." They called him this because it was true. He was a friend of sinners." Jonathan Parnell

Prayer: Jesus, Friend of sinners…I come to You now and ask that You would stir my heart to be a friend of sinners too, just like You. Open my eyes to see those around me who need to know You. They are sick but I know the cure and that cure is You. Help me to not shy away from being around those who are lost or even worse, help me not to judge them because they are lost. May my time with them lead to a saving knowledge of You, Jesus. I ask this in Your powerful and mighty Name, Amen.

Further Scripture Reading:

Mark 2:13-17

Worship: Jesus Friend of Sinners by Casting Crown

# Day 66

"Surely there is not a righteous man on earth who does good and never sins." Ecclesiastes 7:20 (ESV)


"I can't be used by God because of my past."

"I have too many issues in my life to make a difference in this world for Christ."

"I'm afraid I'll mess-up again."

Have you ever said anything that resembles the statements above? If so, it sounds to me like you have counted yourself out of being useful to God because of your past, your present, or your future. You're not alone…a lot of people feel like that. Somewhere down the line you decided that you had to be perfect in order for God to use you for His Kingdom. You decided that because you have flaws, God isn't interested in what you have to offer. Well, I'm about to make you feel sooooo much better about yourself…ya ready? In Matthew chapter 1, a genealogy was written to show who was in the line of Jesus Christ. Now, I know what you're thinking, "This genealogy will be full of sinless, perfect angels." Think again.

The following is a list of some of those not~so~perfect relatives of Jesus Christ. It kind of reads like a Days of Our Lives episode.

*Abraham was a liar.

*Jacob lied and deceived his own father.

*Tamar tricked her father-in-law into sleeping with her.

*Rahab was a prostitute.

*David was an adulterer who covered is affair with murder.

*Solomon was an idolater.

*Manasseh sacrificed his own son for witchcraft and on many different accounts shed innocent blood.

Those are only some of the names in the line of Jesus. I told you they'd rival any soap opera! Let's be honest here, Jesus' family was a hot mess. I've often wondered why the Lord just didn't tell Matthew to leave all of those names out. Why didn't He instruct Matthew to only leave in the names of the people that were actually good? Well, then there would be no hope for any of us. We'd take one look at that genealogy and think,

"I'm out…there's no room in that line of perfection for messed up me!" Instead, God led Matthew to leave those names in and doing so, revealed that He isn't looking for perfection…He's looking for surrender. If you are under the impression that God only uses perfect people, just take one more look at the list above. God only uses flawed people because that's the only kind of people there are. Flawed and messed up. With bad pasts who are struggling in the present and with questionable futures. Beloved, God doesn't need your perfection…He just needs your surrendered heart. You may be used as part of a story of someone's redemption. You may very well be in their line…the line that leads them to Christ. Don't sit out, thinking you don't deserve to be in that story. If you'll let Him, He can use you just like He used all of those other people in the line of our Savior. Quit counting yourself out and start asking God whose line of redemption He can use you in.

Question of the day: Have you counted yourself out of being used by God? If so, why?

Quote of the day: "God uses imperfect people who are in imperfect situations to do His perfect will." David Young

Prayer: Lord, I choose to stop counting myself out of being used by You because of my past, present, or even my future. Thank You for using imperfect, flawed people like me. I desire for You to write me in someone's line of redemption. Use me to help guide their way however You see fit. I believe You for it, I trust You for it, in Jesus Name, Amen.

Further Scripture Reading:

Matthew 1:1-17

# Day 67

"Jesus said, Take ye away the stone. Martha, the sister of him that was dead, saith unto him, Lord, by this time he stinketh." John 11:39 (KJV)

Dead things stinketh, don't they? I remember one time when I was a teenager, my mom was making breakfast. There was a very bad smell coming from the kitchen…and it wasn't her cooking. She was using the toaster and ya'll…there was a DEAD MOUSE up in there! We were toasting *it* AND the bread! Ughhhh! Dead things definitely stink. Do you have dead things in your life? Maybe it's a dream of yours that has died. Maybe it's your marriage that has suffered a death and it just isn't alive anymore. Maybe you put to death a gift or a talent that you *used* to walk in but don't anymore. Even though Lazarus, Martha's brother, had been dead and stunk, Jesus raised him from the dead. It didn't matter that he stunk. It didn't matter that he was dead. Jesus brought Lazarus from death to life. Jesus resurrects dead things. It's what He does. He wants to do the same for you, Beloved. He wants to resurrect the dream you've laid to rest. He wants to resurrect your marriage and bring it to abundant life. He wants to revive the gifts and talents that you have let die. Dead things stinketh…like toasted mice…but resurrected things have a beautiful aroma of life and hope.

Question of the day: What dead things does Jesus want to resurrect in you?

Quote of the day: "Lazarus, come out!" Jesus

Prayer: Jesus, I believe that you raised Lazarus from the dead and that You Yourself were raised from the grave. You are the resurrection and the life. I ask today that You would breathe life into the places I desperately need resurrection. Call them out just like You did Lazarus and watch them walk out of their tomb, full of life. Whether the dead thing in my life was caused by me or someone else, if You haven't put it to death then I receive it's revival. Thank You for making dead things live again. Thank You Jesus for Your resurrecting power! I ask this in the life-giving and powerful Name of Jesus of Nazareth, Amen.

Further Scripture Reading:

John 11:25-26

Philippians 3:10

# Day 68

"They sought God eagerly, and he was found by them. So the LORD gave them rest on every side."
2 Chronicles 15:15b

Ever felt like you were on a hamster wheel? You know, running and running but not going anywhere. Funny, I feel the same way when I'm on a treadmill, but that's not the point. So often we are just spinning our wheels, exhausting ourselves, and wearing ourselves out to the point of giving up. We hit the floor running, full tilt, never stopping to rest. How wonderful would it be to have rest on every side like our Scripture talks about? The parental side: rest. The work side: rest. The marriage side: rest. The physical side: rest. The emotional side: rest. Sounds magical, doesn't it? Well, honestly there is no magic to it. There will be times in your life where when you seek God eagerly, He will give you rest. Your job is to seek, His job is to give. But when He gives, you must receive. It's not saying, "Well...let me finish this one last thing" or "I HAVE to be the one to make this happen correctly". Simply accept the gift of rest, for that is exactly what it is. Our lives our crazy-busy, trust me I know, but God desires to give us rest. If you are tired (and let's face it, who isn't?) ask God to give you rest on every side and then settle into that rest. It's a gift. Plus, it's way better than running on that treadmill…ummmmm…I mean that hamster wheel.

Question of the day: If you are tired and worn out, will you ask God to give you rest today?

Quote of the day: "Rest time is not waste time. It is economy to gather fresh strength…It is wisdom to take occasional furlough. In the long run, we shall do more by sometimes doing less." Charles Spurgeon

Prayer: Heavenly Father, I'm tired. You know it and I know it. I come to You, eagerly asking for rest on every side. I receive it and am thankful for the kind of rest You give. It's full, refreshing, peaceful, and it allows me to catch my breath. Thank You, Father, I love You so, so much. I ask this in Jesus Name, Amen.

Further Scripture Reading:

Psalm 62:1

Matthew 11:28-30

# Day 69

"Let us fix our eyes on Jesus, the author and perfecter of our faith..." Hebrews 12:2

Anyone who knows me at all will not be surprised that I am an author. Why? Well, because I have a lot of words. A *lot* of words. There is something powerful and significant that happens when I take those words that have been dancing in my head and in my heart and pour them out on paper. I can't really describe what it does for me...it's just who I am. An author. I'm not the only one though. There is a Master Author who is writing a story even now. The Author is God and the story is yours. I can see Him writing each chapter of your life. Every chapter is different and every paragraph carefully written. Sometimes it can feel like He's writing a drama, sometimes it feels like a comedy, and other times it feels like a mystery. But actually what He is authoring is your faith journey. He is the author, the originator, of your faith from the moment you say yes to Him. I love that the scripture also says that He's the perfecter or the finisher of our faith. God doesn't start writing the faith journey of your life and then give up on the story half-way through. Nope, not this Author. He perfects and finishes the story all the way to the end. With every stroke of His pen, He is writing for you a hope-full, grace-full, and purposed-full life story. Your story. His story through you. I know your tendency…because it's my tendency too…to tell God He's not doing a good enough job writing your faith story. You are pretty sure you could do a better job yourself. You are convinced that if you were the author of your own story, you'd write it differently. Better. I understand, I really do, but I have come to the realization that I've only had this one lifetime to learn how to navigate my story…God has been doing it since the beginning of time. He's much better at it than I am. Let Him write your story of faith…it will become *His*tory. Your story isn't finished until He writes "The End" which is actually "The Beginning". Trust Him to write a better story than you can. From one author to another Author…I'm glad He's writing mine.

The ~~End~~ Beginning.

Question of the day: Are you letting God write your life story or are you trying to do it on your own?

Quote of the day: "God is still writing your story. Stop trying to steal the pen." Unknown

Prayer: Father, You are the author and the perfecter of my faith story and I give you sole ownership of the pen in order to do so. When I try to take the pen out of your hand because I think I can write a better story, remind me that You are a much better author than I will ever be. Write Your story in me, through me, and for me, God. I trust You in Jesus Name, Amen.

Further Scripture Readings:

Psalm 139:16

Proverbs 3:5-6

# Day 70

"A father to the fatherless, a defender of widows, is God in his holy dwelling. God sets the lonely in families, he leads out the prisoners with singing; but the rebellious live in a sun-scorched land."
Psalm 68:5-6

Lindsey and I have some precious friends, Derek and Michele, who have walked through the journey of adoption. Their story is filled with miracles, difficult decisions, faith-building trust, and a beautiful little "pearl" from India. Adoption. It was never on their radar until God put it there. I can tell you from first-hand experience, once God put it there, there was no going back. There was no way they could walk away from adoption...even if they wanted to...and to be honest, there were probably days they *did* want to. Their journey was amazing and oh what a story of love it has become. God, setting the lonely in families because He is a good, good, Father. Why is adoption so near and dear to God's heart? The answer is pretty simple. God has adopted us. His adoption of us is the purest picture of love ever depicted. When we say yes to

Him, He makes us one of His *own* children. We have the same rights as if we were born into the Kingdom. But we weren't. We weren't born into the Kingdom, but we were loved enough to be *brought into* it. Imagine someone rescuing you from death. He swoops down right in the nick of time and saves you from dying. He cleans you up, wipes your wounds, maybe even feeds you a meal. Then he looks at you and says, "Well, I've saved you from death. Now, off you go! Have a great day!" You'd be forever grateful to your rescuer, wouldn't you? Now imagine that same scenario only instead of sending you on your way, He looks at you and says, "I know this must have been a terrible ordeal for you. I'd like to adopt you into my family and be your father forever. You will never want for anything ever again because I am the richest person alive. Let's go change your last name, my child." See, God didn't just rescue you; He rescued you AND adopted you. Let that sink in for a minute. Adoption in the natural is powerful because adoption in the supernatural has always been God's plan. A Father to the fatherless and the one who sets the lonely in families...that's my Daddy...and He's yours too.

Question of the day:  How does knowing that you've been adopted by God make you feel?

Quote of the day:  "If anybody understands God's ardor for his children, it's someone who has rescued an orphan from despair, for that is what God has done for us. God has adopted you. God sought you, found you, signed the papers and took you home."  Max Lucado

Prayer:  Lord, how thankful I am to You for adopting me!  Help me to never get over the fact that You have claimed me as Your child!  I'm reminded that the gospel is not a picture of adoption but adoption is a picture of the gospel!  I love You Abba, Father!  I pray this in Jesus Name, Amen.

Further Scripture Readings:

Galatians 4:4-6

Romans 8:16-17

Worship:  I am a Child of God by Hillsong

# Day 71

"The only thing that matters is faith expressing itself through love." Galatians 5:6

Our Ladies Life Group took cookies to the surrounding fire stations one Spring. You would have thought we had given them a million dollars instead of a tray full of Nestle Toll House cookies! They were so thankful and so very overwhelmed by this small act of love. Not too long after that, a terrible hurricane hit Florida and our little town had an exorbitant amount of evacuees. The lines at the gas pumps were mind-blowing. Our town was running out of gas, water bottles, and patience. I was in the store when I learned that one of our local churches had scheduled hot meals to be served that night for evacuees and another church was offering their building for people to stay in for a few days. I was walking out of Ingles feeling a bit sorry for myself because I had to wait in line for gas earlier AND the only water bottles in stock were the pricey ones. As I got to my car, I noticed that there was a truck that had two dogs in travel cages in its bed and next to the truck there was a large van. Both vehicles had Florida license plates. There was a large family gathered around the two vehicles. The mom was making peanut butter and jelly sandwiches out of the van and handing them to her kids to eat in the parking lot. I wanted to crumble. The severity of their situation hit me like a mac truck. I began speaking to them and they shared their story of packing everything they could, including their dogs, and driving their two vehicles away from their house, not knowing if it would be there when they got back. I shared with them that one church was offering free meals and another was offering lodging. Then I prayed for them, right there in the Ingles parking lot. All five of their children held hands and the mama began to cry. She said she had been praying for God's provision for their family and she was overwhelmed by His goodness. See, *nothing else matters* except our faith expressing itself in love. Nothing else matters. *Nothing.* Our faith in Jesus Christ should extend itself out in the form of us loving others. Who cares if we have faith if we never allow it to show itself in the form of loving and caring for one another? Our faith should transform us into walking, living, breathing, executers of love. Loving others doesn't have to cost a lot...a tray of chocolate chip cookies for fire fighters or a free hot meal to evacuees…but what *they* see is God's love acted out through our faith. That's what matters. More than anything.

Question of the day: How has your faith expressed itself through love?

Quote of the day: "Love that goes upward is worship; Love that goes outward is affection; Love that stoops is grace." Donald Barnhouse

Prayer: Father, help my faith to express itself through love because that is what You say matters the most! Open my eyes to see how I can walk this way and may I be a vessel of functioning love to others so they may see You. I love you and thank You for the opportunities You will bring my way! I pray this in Jesus Name, Amen.

Further Scripture Reading:

1 Corinthians 13:1-13

# Day 72

"It is for freedom that Christ has set us free. Stand firm, then, and do not let yourselves be burdened again by a yoke of slavery." Galatians 5:1

I watched a quick video on Facebook the other day with the Christian vocalist Lauren Daigle. She had visited Statesville Correctional Prison and the video showed her on stage with some other vocalists in the background. She is singing the song, <u>How can it be</u> and the line says, "You say that I am free, how can it be?" Ya'll...she's in a *prison.* I was wondering if she saw the irony in it all? The video shows all of the other vocalists in the background crying, wiping their faces, as the tears rolled down. You can hear the prisoners singing. You could literally feel the presence of God in that moment. I pondered this scene for awhile. This room full of prisoners were able to sing, "You plead my cause, You right my wrongs, You break my chains, You overcome. You say that I am free, how can it be?" Prisoners, free? That really doesn't make sense. I began to settle into the thought that you don't have to be behind bars in a prison to be a prisoner. In fact, that day showed me that there are people in prison who are more free than some of us walking around outside of those prison walls. Those men didn't feel shackled or enslaved. Those men didn't feel like prisoners. They were free and that freedom was liberating. Us, on the other hand? Well, some of us are prisoners...we just can't see the bars. Some of us are prisoners to fear. Some are prisoners to pride. Others are prisoners of people's opinions. Anxiety is a horrible prison. So is insecurity. The shackles and chains that bind us don't need a prison cell, they just need a prisoner. Oh Beloved, God doesn't want you to be imprisoned. He sent His Son to set you free. God desires for your chains and your shackles to fall to the ground, breaking any hold over you. He wants you to walk in the freedom He has to offer. If a prisoner behind bars can experience true freedom, so can you, Beloved, so can you.

Question of the day: What are you a prisoner to?

Quote of the day: "Live free or die: Death is not the worst of evils." General John Stark

Prayer: Father God, I confess my tendency to be a prisoner and I ask that You show me how to walk in freedom. You sent Your Son to die so I could be free and I want that freedom in my life. Shackles and chain may no longer have a hold on me and I declare that I am free in Jesus Name! I pray this in the only Name that breaks the chains, Jesus, Amen!

Further Scripture Reading:

Psalm 119:45

John 8:36

Worship: How can it be by Lauren Daigle

# Day 73

"...Or do we need, like some people, letters of recommendations to you or from you? You yourselves are our letter, written on our hearts, known and read by everybody. You show that you are a letter from Christ, the result of our ministry, written not with ink but with the Spirit of the living God, not on tablets of stone, but on tablets of human hearts. " 2 Corinthians 3:2


I graduated from UGA (go Dawgs!) in December and took a long-term substitute job teaching fifth grade. Fifth grade was and adventure...to say the least. One boy threw a pencil at me. One girl said that she wanted her other teacher back. One boy wouldn't talk at all. To say I had my work cut out for me was the understatement of the year. I worked very hard at loving them, listening to them, teaching them, and bringing out the best in them. It wasn't an easy feat but eventually I began to see the tide change. As the year came to a close, I received a sealed envelope in my teacher box. I opened it. And cried. One of the parents had written a letter of recommendation for me to the Superintendent. This father shared that his son had made the most remarkable progress in the few months that I was his teacher. He told the Superintendent that I would be a great asset to their school system and that he should hire me for the upcoming year. Ya'll…this letter of recommendation slayed me. That was over twenty years ago but I still remember it so vividly. God has used this story many times in my life to remind me of the Scripture above. We are walking letters of recommendation for Christ. People read us daily and decide whether or not they will give God a try. Wikipedia defines a letter of recommendation as a document where the writer assesses the qualities, characteristics, and capabilities of the person being recommended in terms of that individual's ability to perform a particular task. If people were to "read" your life, would they want the God that you profess? Your life assess the qualities, characteristics, and capabilities of *God* in terms of His ability to perform a particular task…and the task is saving, caring, and loving those He created. If someone were to read your life right now, would God get the job?

Question of the day:  When others "read" your life, what will they learn about God?

Quote of the day: "People draw their picture of God from the actions of Christians, and our lives should paint a picture of who He is."  Bruce Goettsche

Prayer:  Father, I am Your walking letter of recommendation.  When people read my life, may they see Your goodness, Your love, Your salvation, and Your faithfulness.  Help me to be a glowing recommendation of who You are and may it bring others closer to You in Jesus Name, Amen.

Further Scripture Reading:

2 Corinthians 3:1-6

# Day 74

"Set a guard over my mouth, LORD; keep watch over the door of my lips." Psalm 141:3

One day when my middle child was about three years old, we were driving in the car just chatting away. I was telling her something that I thought was important and she responded, "I don't care." I quickly scolded her and said, "It's disrespectful to tell me you don't care. You owe me an apology." Silence. Complete silence. I took a deep breath because I figured this may be a battle of the wills. What she didn't know about this battle is that I had waaaayyyy more years of experience in being stubborn than she did...I would no doubt win! But...then I heard that sweet little three-year-old voice, who still couldn't pronounce her "r's" very well, say, "I'm sowwy....**I still don't care**...but I'm sowwy." This was one of those moments where I felt like she was holding up a mirror in front of my face...because all I saw was MYSELF! This is something I totally would have said! The verse above really paints a picture for me. I see my mouth with a huge padlock on it and an eensy weensy little man dressed as a guard sitting on the padlock. I need both of those to insure that what comes out of my mouth is acceptable. Here's a novel thought…just because I think it doesn't mean I have to say it! The power of life and death are in the tongue yet we tend to let our words flow with ease, no matter the carnage we leave behind. Our words matter. What we say matters. Not just to others but to God too. I've heard people say on many occasions, "I just tell it like it is, I can't help it!" or "I'm just brutally honest, it's how I was made!" Honestly, most of the time phrases like this are just an excuse for people not keeping a guard over their mouths or a watch over their lips. There's a story in the Bible where a bunch of soldiers came to arrest Jesus. Peter was so angry that he pulled out his sword and cut off a soldier's ear. I'm still not sure if he meant to cut the guy's head off and just missed or what? Anyway, instead of Jesus high-fiving Peter because of what he did, Jesus walked over to the soldier, bent down, picked up the guy's bloody, gross, ear and put it back on his head. This is what happens when I use my words carelessly. I walk around chopping off ears and Jesus has to go behind me, picking them up and sticking them back on. We don't have the luxury of "telling it like it is" *no matter what.* We don't own the right to say whatever we want to say because it makes *us* feel better. We are accountable for the things that come out of our mouth. We need to ask God to give us that eensy weensy little man dressed as a guard and that padlock and set it over our mouths. You don't like that idea? I'm sorry. I still don't care, but I'm sorry.

Question of the day: Do you guard what comes out of your mouth?

Quote of the day: "Words are like eggs dropped from great heights; you can no more call them back than ignore the mess they leave when they fall." Jodi Picoult

Prayer: Lord I am specifically asking you to set a guard over my mouth and keep watch over the door of my lips. I confess that I allow things to flow from my mouth that I shouldn't. Help me to remember that my words matter. I am asking You for Your help in Jesus Name, Amen.

Further Scripture Reading:

Proverbs 12:18

Ephesians 4:29

# Day 75

"If it is possible, as far as it depends on you, live at peace with everyone." Romans 12:18

I love to laugh and Sinbad makes me laugh until my belly hurts! I grew up watching the comedian on TV and just the other day I watched a YouTube video of him. My guy called in the middle of me watching it and I couldn't get myself together from all the laughing. Sinbad was telling a story of how two young adults met, fell in love, and were going to get married. They were all goo-goo and gaa-gaa about each other and neither of them could do any wrong in the other's eyes. The day came for them to get married and as they looked lovingly at one another, they said "I do". As soon as the preacher announced that they were husband and wife, the new wife whips her head around at her man and with her eyes bulging, her face tight, and her voice harsh, she growls, "Some thangs gotta change up in here!" That new wife had plans to make some changes in her new husband and apparently wanted to start on those changes as soon as possible! I can pretty much guarantee that no matter how hard she worked to change him, she was going to fail. Why? Well,

229

first, it's not her job to change anyone. Second, people will not change until they are ready to. Her nagging may get him to pick up his dirty clothes but that doesn't mean she changed him…she just changed his *behavior* temporarily. She may criticize his political views until he stops talking about it but she didn't change *him*. When we try to change other people, what we are really doing is trying to "fix" them. The problem is, just because they don't do it the way we want them to, does not mean they need to be <u>fixed</u>. It just means they do it differently than YOU want them to do it. When we want to see a change in a person, it usually has to do with a habit we don't like or a character trait that bothers *us*. Sometimes, when we try to change someone, it is birthed out of a selfish desire, not out of the desire to help *them*. We want them to do what *we* want them to do. Now, sometimes we desire to see a change in a person because they are heading down the wrong path. This desire is an unselfish one of course, but the truth remains the same, you can't change them or their heart. Whether it is a habit, a character trait, or if they are heading down the wrong path, when it comes to changing or fixing them, hear me loud and clear…it is not our job. It is not our job. Once again, it is not our job. Any change that happens within a person comes from the surrender within them coupled alongside the power of God. God is the only one powerful enough to change the heart of a person and that person has to be *willing* to change. The only person you can change is YOU. And let's face it, how do <u>you</u> react when someone wants to change you? You dig your heels in the ground, cross your arms, throw your chin in the air and think, "How dare they try to change ME!" You need to stop the nagging, the manipulation, the passive aggressive comments, the silent treatment, or the shutting out because whatever it is they are doing goes against your personal preference. If you really want someone to produce a real change, **pray for them**, constantly. Ask God to do the changing and pray that the person surrenders to the process, wanting the change for themselves too. We live at peace with one another when we realize that it's not our job to change anyone. It's our job to love them. Pray for them. Encourage them. The peace comes from the knowledge that we do not possess the ability, the power, or the wisdom to change someone. But God can. So let Him.

Question of the day: Have you tried to change someone and if so, how did it go?

Quote of the day: "Consider how hard it is to change yourself and you'll understand what little chance you have in trying to change others."
Jacob M. Braude


Prayer: Oh Father, I confess to you that I have often tried to change people because of my own likes and dislikes. Please forgive me for stepping into Your role as God. I commit to leaving it up to You for You have the ability to change hearts and lives. I commit to praying for those who need a heart change. I also choose to stop trying to fix those around me because I don't like what or how they are doing something. I ask for Your help in the strong Name of Jesus of Nazareth, Amen.


Further Scripture Reading:

Ezekiel 36:26

2 Corinthians 5:17

# Day 76

"You are the salt of the earth, but if salt has lost its taste, how shall its saltiness be restored? It is no longer good for anything except to be thrown out and trampled under people's feet." Matthew 5:13

I LOVE to cook…which is quite convenient because I also love to eat! I really do try to make delicious food that my family loves which is sometimes tough because there are five of us and we all have different tastes when it comes to our favorite foods! Unfortunately, I have this horrible tendency when I cook…I over-salt stuff…quite often in fact! I've over-salted roast, mashed potatoes, soup, country fried steak and a myriad of other things. Everyone is really nice about it but by the looks of their full plates and empty bellies, I am quite aware of my salty faux pas. Salt is an interesting little mineral. It's not a spice or an herb so it doesn't lose its flavor. Salt promotes healing and has many health benefits. Salt enhances the flavor of food. Salt makes a difference. So do you. Yes, YOU! You make a difference in this world because *you* are salt. Just as a little salt can go a long way, it only takes a little of your influence in a situation to make a difference. You may think, "But I'm only *ONE* person...how can **I** make a difference?" My answer to your question is Nicholas Winton. Ever heard of him? Most people haven't but to 669 children who were rescued from almost certain death on the eve of World War II, this one man made quite the difference. In 1938, Hitler's army invaded Czechoslovakia and sent 150,000 refugees to Prague. Parents were frantically trying to get their children out of the refugee camps and Winton decided to help. He took on the Nazis and British bureaucracy and laid the foundation to transport the children to Britain on trains. On March 14th, 1939, the first train left Prague carrying 20 children. Six more trains left between March and August of 1939. Because of Nicholas Winton, 669 children were saved and went on to have families of their own. It's estimated that over 6000 people are alive who wouldn't be if Winton hadn't stepped in to make a difference. One man made a difference. It is the power of one. Our lives *can* make a difference. In Ezekiel 22:30 God says, "I looked for someone who might rebuild the wall of righteousness that guards the land. I searched for someone to stand in the gap in the wall so I wouldn't have to destroy the land, but I found no *one*". (emphasis mine) You have what it takes to make a difference in this world because God created you to do that very thing. Jesus would not have declared you "salt" if He didn't think you were capable of making an impact on those around you. Start looking for ways to make a difference and start bringing your salt to the table.

Question of the day: Do you believe that you can make a difference in this world? Why or why not?

Quote of the day: "One person at a time, one day at a time, and one project at a time, you can make a difference that will leave a lasting impact on the world." Asad Meah

Prayer: Father God, I don't often believe that I have the ability to make a difference in this huge world. Your Son has called me salt so I choose to pick up that calling and make an impact on those You have called me to. Help my eyes to see and my ears to hear when I am to step in and add my salt to a situation. Thank You for the reminder that I am not here on earth just to live and to die. Instead, I am to make an impact on those around me. Thank You Jesus and I pray this in Your Name, Amen.

Further Scripture Reading:

John 6:1-14

# Day 77

"Do what the LORD your God commands and follow his teachings. Obey everything written in the Law of Moses. Then you will be a success, no matter what you do or where you go." 1 Kings 2:3

I asked my dad one day how he defined success. Honestly, I expected his answer to be "a big house" or "a nice car". But his answer slayed me. He said, "To me, success is when my kids need a new pair of shoes, I can go buy them." No mention of a big house or a nice car. It got me to thinking…how do we define success? Is it a destination or a pursuit? How much money defines "success" and who gets to define what success really is anyway? I know, it's a lot of questions but I couldn't help it, success seemed so…so…well, so subjective. The verse above is actually a conversation King David had with his son, Solomon. King David is about to die and he desires to impart one last piece of knowledge to his son. He tells Solomon to obey God and follow His teachings and that if he does, he will be a success no matter what he does or where he goes. Solomon heeded his dad's advice. When God came to Solomon in a dream, He said, "Ask for whatever you want me to give you." Hmmmm…what would you have asked for? A yacht? To win the lottery? A mansion? How about a lifetime supply of Chic-fil-a? (oh, sorry…this was your list, not mine) Guess what Solomon asked for? He asked for a wise and discerning heart. Once again, no "big house", no "nice car". The Lord rewarded his request by granting Solomon a wise and discerning heart but He didn't stop there. He also gave him what he didn't ask for…both riches and honor. Success. Here's what it looked like for Solomon:

Solomon was anointed King of Israel.

God appeared to Solomon two times.

Solomon authored 3,000 proverbs and composed 1,005 songs; he was a botanist and biologist, and owned 1,400 chariots and 12,000 horses.

He received 666 talents of gold yearly. That's about 730,000 ounces of gold per year.

Solomon built the magnificent Lord's Temple in Jerusalem, which housed the Ark of the Covenant. The construction of this temple was Solomon's greatest career accomplishment.

"King Solomon was greater in riches and wisdom than all the other kings of the earth." (1 Kings 10:23).

He wrote three books of the Bible: Song of Songs, Proverbs, and Ecclesiastes.

This dude had it going on, didn't he? But here's the thing…at the end of his reign, Solomon wrote Ecclesiastes and he summarized his life for those who were following him, kind of like being on Twitter or Instagram. This is what he said, "Now all has been heard; here is the conclusion of the matter: Fear God and keep his commandments, for this is the whole duty of man." Ecclesiastes 12:13 Does that sound familiar? This is pretty much what his dad had told him before he died. Solomon followed his dad's advice and in doing so, experienced a huge amount of success but it all boiled down to one thing…obeying God. Obeying what God says. Doing what He is asking of you. This leads to success. Maybe not a bazillion dollars and maybe not even a new car, but when you obey God, His eyes view you as successful. Obeying God equals hitting the lottery. Ask Solomon, he'll tell you…so will my dad.

Question of the day: How do you define success?

Quote of the day: "On earth we have nothing to do with success or its results, but only being true to God and for God; for it is sincerity and not success which is the sweet savor before God." Frederick W. Robertson

Prayer: Lord, I often forget that success is not my main goal or focus…obedience to You is. Help me to obey Your Word and Your way. You desire my obedience, not my success. I trust that You have what is best for me and I desire to walk in all that You have ordained. I thank You for who You are, in Jesus Name, Amen.

Further Scripture Reading:
Joshua 1:8
Psalm 1:1~6

# Day 78

"For My thoughts are not your thoughts, nor are
your ways My ways," declares the LORD.
"For as the heavens are higher than the earth, so
are My ways higher than your ways and My
thoughts than your thoughts." Isaiah 55:8-9

A few years ago, the Lord led our family to move
about two hours away from where we lived and
where I had grown up. I didn't *want* to go but I
knew God was asking us to go, so we went. The
Lord was faithful in settling us into a beautiful
home in a great town. The first year was tough on
all of us. One kid cried every Sunday night
because she had to go to a school that was still so
new to her. One kid would throw up on my
kitchen floor weekly and had anxiety attacks. And
one kid figured he *should* be upset because his
sisters were and so he would cry too. I wasn't
much better. I wanted to go home. Bad. A couple
of years had passed and as much as I wanted to
move back home, the Lord continued to shut doors
to do so until one day, a job opportunity landed in
our laps. They sought my husband out for this job
and approached him with this opportunity to

move close to home. I was ecstatic to say the least. Home. Just that word brought such joy to my soul. I began to look for houses, called realtors, even picked out curtains for our new bedroom! In my heart, I was already back home. Then Lindsey called me one morning and let me know that they had decided to go a different route and they weren't going to hire him. I was devastated. I bellowed. I cried. I sobbed. Was I disappointed in God? The churchy answer would be, "All things work together for the good of those who love him" but the **real** answer, *MY* answer, was yes, 100%, I was disappointed in God. Guess what? He can handle it. God is able to handle my disappointment…pouting and all. I was disappointed that He didn't deliver on what I thought He should have delivered on. I was disappointed that He didn't answer the way I thought we would. I was disappointed in Him. I can hear some of you now, "I'm appalled! How dare she be disappointed in God!" I know, it sounds so, so, well…human, doesn't it? Newsflash…I am human, and so are you. Was God mad at me for how I felt? Nope. Wanna know what He did? He listened to my disappointment, my anguish, my cries…and then He gently reminded me that He loved me and He was in control of it all. Did His words evaporate my despair or disintegrate my disappointment? No, they didn't. But what they did do was remind me that I have a trustworthy Abba who is for me. It took me a very long while to recover from my disappointment of not getting to move back home. Each time I began to feel that overwhelming sense of despair, I was reminded that He cares and He will do what He sees is best...and that at the end of the day, the week, or the year, He is faithful and I can trust Him.

Question of the day: Have you ever been disappointed in God? If so, how did you handle it?

Quote of the day: "Never be afraid to trust an unknown future to a known God." Corrie Ten Boom

Prayer: Lord, help me to remember when I feel disappointed in You and how You chose to handle something in my life, that I can trust You with everything. Everything. You are trustworthy and even though I may not understand what You are doing or why, help me to trust Your heart for me. I love and trust You, Jesus, and in Your Name I pray, Amen.

Further Scripture Reading:

Psalm 34:18

Philippians 4:6-7

Worship: Thy Will by Hillary Scott

# Day 79

"Then Peter got down out of the boat, walked on the water and came toward Jesus." Matthew 14:29

Out of everyone in the Bible, I relate to Peter the most. He was a little feisty (remember when he cut the ear of the soldier?) and he denied Jesus three times even after Jesus warned him he would. After Jesus died, Peter was so discouraged and scared that he quit being a disciple and went back to fishing because it was what he knew. Once Jesus gently restored him, Peter became unstoppable for the cause of Christ and at the end of his life, he was killed for his Savior. I can relate to him the most because he was a hot mess but he sure loved his friend, Jesus…and so do I. One of the stories I left out from above was when Peter and some of the disciples were in a boat on a lake. Just before dawn, Jesus walked on the water toward the boat. Everyone started freaking out (seriously, wouldn't you?) and Jesus called out and told them not to be afraid. Then, my boy Pete says, "Lord if it's You, tell me to come on the water." Pete's awesome. Once Jesus says, "Come", Peter got out of the boat and walked to Jesus. Now see, this is where it all comes apart for most people. They start talking about how little faith Peter had when he saw the wind and the waves. They fuss about how he got distracted and needed Jesus to save him. Poor Pete…he gets a bad rap in my opinion. Wanna know how I see it? Peter got out of the boat, ya'll. He was literally the only other person in history besides Jesus to walk on water. He had enough faith and confidence in Jesus to throw his leg over the side of that boat and walk. On water. I think he deserves some props for that, don't you? There was no mention of anyone else in that boat throwing their leg over the side, only Peter. Peter had a lot of flaws, don't we all, but I believe that he trusted his Savior. Did Peter look at the waves around him and begin to fall? Yes, he did. But Jesus quickly stepped in to save Peter, just like He does for us. The truth of the matter is that Peter got distracted by all that was happening around him while he was on the water. So much so that it caused him to falter. But let me tell you what I love the most about Pete…he had enough faith to get out of the boat. He got out of the boat so he could walk on water. And he did. I desire to have the same "leg-over-the-side-of-the-boat" faith as Peter did.  What about you?  Are you a boat-sitter or a water-walker?

Question of the day:  Would you have stayed in the boat or thrown your leg over the side to walk on water?  Why?

Quote of the day:  "Getting out of the boat was Peter's great gift to Jesus; the experience of walking on water was Jesus' great gift to Peter." John Ortburg

Prayer:  Lord, I want to be like Peter.  I want to have enough faith in You to get out of the boat and walk on water.  Speak deep courage and faith into my spirit even now.  I can only imagine the look on Your face, Jesus, as You watched Your friend, Your disciple, step out of the boat and do the very same thing You were doing.  No one else would, but Peter did.  Help me to do walk in that same faith, even if no one else does.  I choose to be a water-walker, Jesus.  I ask this in the miraculous Name of Jesus, the one who walked on water, Amen.


Further Scripture Reading:

Mark 14:22-33

# Day 80

"My sheep listen to my voice; I know them, and they follow me." Matthew 10:27

Some of you may know my story, some of you may not. It's a story I NEVER get tired of telling. It's a story that I still can't believe God gave me. Ya ready? In July of 2016 I was in my pool, just spending some time with the Lord which was pretty normal for me. It's quiet, calm, and I feel like I can hear Him speak...as clear as the water. I now call my pool, the Pool of Bethesda, you'll find out why soon. On that day in July, the Lord told me that I needed to make an appointment with my doctor and have my uterus taken out because there were things unseen. I'm not kidding. He actually spoke to me about my uterus. So, I made an appointment and saw the doctor. He said that there were a few issues but nothing pressing. Nothing that required surgery immediately but it was up to me. I shared with Lindsey that we needed to schedule the hysterectomy...the appointment was made for October. As time passed, I began to doubt what I heard from the Lord...because it didn't make sense...who agrees to surgery when the doctor said it wasn't an emergency? Who does that? Me. I do that. Because He said. I had the surgery on October 10th and they found that my uterus was more prolapsed then they thought. There it was...the unseen...or so I thought. I went to the doctor for my one week checkup and after he said everything was healing well, he said, "Now, we have to talk about the pathology report." The pathology report? What? Okay. The doctor then tells me that the pathology report confirmed that I had Uterine Cancer. Uterine Cancer. Cancer. Me. He continued to say that it was in the lining of my uterus and they wouldn't have found it until it was everywhere in there. The standard course of action for Uterine Cancer is a hysterectomy. I already had one. Because HE told me to. The doctor was confident that it was contained. I was confident in HIM. I re-read the journal entry I wrote when I was struggling with whether or not I heard Him about this "get your uterus out" thing...and this is what God said to me that day. "You heard me. Don't doubt it. I spoke. I see you. I see ALL things. Trust me with this....it will be worth it. You will see. You will see me in this. I am loving. I am faithful. I am for you. I will guard you. I will protect you. You are mine." Later in the journal entry He says,

"Trust me. Trust this process. Trust what you know you heard. There is something bigger at work here." Ya'll...seriously...isn't He a good, good Father. I am *still* overwhelmed. And grateful. And overwhelmed. He knew I had cancer. Want to know why? Because He made me....because I am fearfully and wonderfully made and He sees me. Sometimes God asks people to walk through the journey of cancer...the whole journey...the rough, terrible journey. Sometimes He allows that journey to look a bit different as He did with me. The purpose of both journeys is exactly the same...to glorify God. So, I glorify Him with all of my being. I point to Him. He is tender. He is loving. He is enough. God cured my cancer before the doctors ever even knew there was any cancer. Don't ever doubt that The Good Shepherd doesn't speak to His sheep…His sheep just have to listen. I'm so glad I did.

Question of the day: Do you believe that God speaks to His children?

Quote of the day: "A word from Jesus changed everything." Henry T. Blackaby

Prayer: Father, I know You speak and I want to hear You. Remove every distraction that would hinder the ears of my heart to hear what You would say to me. I desire to hear every whisper and every word You speak to me. Help me to hear You and obey, even if it doesn't make sense to me. I will do this because I trust You. Thank You for loving me enough to speak to me…I love You and I pray this in the powerful Name of Jesus of Nazareth, Amen.

Further Scripture Reading:

Genesis 5:9-24

# Day 81

"When Jesus saw their faith, He said to the man, "Friend, your sins are forgiven." Luke 5:20

Great friends are hard to find, aren't they? In fact, I dare say that great friends only come around a few times in our lifetime. What do you think makes a great friend? I remember a very long time ago when a boy had broken my heart. My best friend showed up unannounced at my front door with a gallon of ice cream and a bag of Starburst. I was lying in the bed with all my clothes on and really didn't want to get up…but I couldn't let the ice cream melt! I've had friends make me meals when I was sick or had surgery. I've had friends who would pray for me without ceasing. I have this one best friend, Betsy, who is a baby whisperer and there were countless nights when I would take my screaming little guy to her house, hand him over to her, and lie down and go to sleep on her couch. My nurse friend, Heather, was always my go-to when I needed nursing advice. Faithful friends are a gift. Here's a question…what kind of friend are *you*? The verse above comes from a story in the New Testament where Jesus was speaking to a lot of people in a house. There was a man who was paralyzed and lying on a mat. His friends were carrying him and trying to get him in to see Jesus because they knew Jesus could heal the man. They couldn't find a way in the house because of all the people and it was so crowded. Some friends would have said, "Buddy, we're sorry, we tried. Maybe next time." Or maybe, "Friend, we are going to leave you outside the house, maybe Jesus will see you and heal you later." Nope. Not these faithful friends. Do you know what they did? They climbed on the roof while carrying their friend on his mat. They made a hole in the roof and lowered their friend down in front of Jesus! Now, those are some friends! Notice what Jesus said when he saw the paralyzed man, "When Jesus saw their faith, He said to the man, "Friend, your sins are forgiven." Whose faith did Jesus notice? The paralytic's? Nope. It was the faith of the friends that moved Jesus to heal him. Guess what else? Jesus forgave the man's sin first, then healed his body. The friends that were faithful enough to lower him from the roof actually had a part in saving his soul. Are you this kind of friend? The kind of friend that would go the extra mile to make sure your friend meets Jesus? The kind of friend that makes a way to ensure that your friend is whole...mind, body, and spirit? Would you scale a roof so your friend could meet Jesus?

Question of the day: What kind of friend are you?

Quote of the day: "A true friend unbosoms freely, advises justly, assists readily, adventures boldly, takes all patiently, defends courageously, and continues a friend unchangeably." William Penn

Prayer: Father God, help me to be a faithful friend to those You have placed in my life. Show me their needs and use me as a vessel of Your healing and provision. I love my friends and I desire them to be whole in You. I trust You for it, I believe You for it in Jesus Name, Amen.

Further Scripture Reading:
Luke 5:17-39

# Day 82

"The godly may trip seven times, but they will get up again." Proverbs 24:16 (NLT)

In 1997, the alternative music group, Chumbawamba released a song called, "I get knocked down". The lead vocalist sings in his English accent, "I get knocked down, but I get up again. You're never gonna keep me down." I honestly believe that this could be my theme song. The anthem for my spiritual life. I get knocked down. I mess up. I fail. I slide face-first into the gravel. But I get up again. The Scripture verse above brings me such hope because God knows we are going to trip but instead of scolding us or wagging His finger at us, He reminds us that we just need to stand up again. The godly (or the righteous as it reads in some translations) will fall down but we don't stay there. We get up, dust ourselves off, and move forward. Don't get so hung up on the fact that you fell. Focus on the fact that you have the ability to get back up and start over again. So many of the people in the Bible experienced times when they fell. They sinned. They messed up. But they didn't stay down. Consider David. He had one of his lead soldiers, Uriah, murdered because David had slept with his wife. An adulterer **AND** a murderer. Talk about falling. But see, here's the thing, David confessed his sins to God, repented of them, and asked God to continue to use him. Here's how I know that David didn't stay down after he fell. David is known in the Bible as a man after God's own heart and there is no caveat that reads "David was a man after God's own heart until he messed up and then he wasn't any more…" It just says that he was. Period. We're going to fall because we are human. But the Bible says that the godly or the righteous will get back up again. I bet David would have liked Chumbawamba's song, don't you? I get knocked down…but I get up again…oh no, now it's stuck in my head. I know what I'll be singing all night…

Question of the day: Can you relate to Chumbawamba's song?

Quote of the day: "Fall seven times. Stand up eight." Japanese Proverb

Prayer: Lord, I know I will stumble and fall because I am human, but please remind me of the necessity of standing back up again. Help me to rise, knowing that You have more work for me to do! Thank You for this reminder God! I love You! I pray this in Jesus Name, Amen.

Further Scripture Reading:

Psalm 51

# Day 83

"A hot-tempered person stirs up conflict, but the one who is patient calms a quarrel." Proverbs 15:13

I was cooking dinner the other night and I was in the middle of making Baked Ziti. If you've never tried it, you're missing out! Anyway, I had the Italian Sausage and sauce simmering on the stove and my next step was to boil the pasta. I like my pasta al dente. I poured salt in the water and turned up the heat to get the boil going. As the water came to a rolling boil, I dumped the pasta into the pot. I promise I only looked away for a few seconds and then before I knew it, the water was boiling over the pot and onto the stovetop! Boy was it a mess and it smelled really baaaaddddl! Then it hit me, that's how it can happen to us too. Not the pasta part but the boiling over part. Our anger can go from 0 to 60 in a blink of an eye and the next thing we know, we are at our boiling point. And here's what I've learned about our boiling point...nothing good happens when we get there! We are all going to have moments when we become angry and just in case you didn't know, anger isn't a sin. It's what we *do* with that anger that can become a sin. I think the thing that can really ruin me when it comes to my "boiling point" is that I often feel like it hits me out of nowhere. It sneaks up on me and then, "WHAM"...I'm done for. Here's what I've been learning...know what your triggers are. For instance, if people who drive "poorly" are what set you off, then make a decision when you get in the car to be aware that it could happen. If a dirty house can make you blow your top, then be ready to call on God for help as soon as you see the dirty socks on the floor for the 4,675 time. You do not have to be controlled by your anger. It does not have to own you. God has equipped you to handle your anger in a much more productive way than to just blow up. You **do not** have to be like my pasta when it boiled over...messy and smelly.

Question of the day: What tends to make you boil?

Quote of the day: "When your temper becomes frayed, your sensibility is in shreds." Anthony T. Hincks

Prayer: Father, I know my tendency to lose my temper and become so angry that I'm at my boiling point. Help me to know when it's happening and help me to surrender it to You. I don't want to be known as a hot-head or quick-tempered. Thank You for seeing me through this and I pray this in the strong Name of Jesus, Amen.

Further Scripture Reading:

Proverbs 14:29

Proverbs 29:22

# Day 84

"So I will restore to you the years that the swarming locust has eaten, the crawling locust, the consuming locust, and the chewing locust..."
Joel 2:25

Bugs are pretty annoying, aren't they? I've often asked God why He made all those little troublesome things anyway. They get in your drink, fly around your head, eat your plants, lay eggs in your trash can...and that's just in the month of June. Maybe that's why some of them are called "June Bugs"? Anyway, I've just never been a big fan of insects. There is one insect that the Bible talks about in the Old Testament. It's a locust and it's similar to the grasshopper. Wikipedia says of these insects, "In the solitary phase, these grasshoppers are innocuous, their numbers are low, and they do not pose a major economic threat to agriculture. However, under suitable conditions of drought followed by rapid vegetation growth, serotonin in their brains triggers a dramatic set of changes: they start to breed abundantly and become gregarious and nomadic when their populations become dense enough. They form bands of wingless nymphs which later become swarms of winged adults. Both the bands and the swarms move around and rapidly strip fields and cause damage to crops." Basically, when there has been a drought followed by an abundant, healthy crop, these insects breed and become flying destroyers of the crops. These bugs eat the harvest. The harvest that was supposed to be on the farmer's table. The harvest that was supposed to pay the bills. The harvest that was supposed to be a reward. Eaten. Destroyed. You might be able to relate. You have had things stolen from you. Eaten. Destroyed. Maybe it was your innocence and childhood. Maybe it was your dreams and plans. Maybe precious people that you loved were taken too soon and you were left damaged and destroyed. Maybe you've watched your child destroy his/her life and feel helpless and hopeless. You've experienced loss, hurt, overwhelming sorrow and deep grief. If you were to take an aerial view of land that had been destroyed by locust, you'd see decimated soil with no living thing in sight. This is how your heart feels. Decimated…with no living thing in sight. You have been robbed and you *feel* every single thing that those locusts stole. Beloved, I need you to hear me when I tell you this…God WILL restore all that the locusts have eaten. HE says that, not me. The things in your life that the locusts have crawled on, consumed, and chewed will be restored, made whole, given back, and repaired. Don't lose heart, dear one. He is God and He is in the business of restoring and renewing. In fact, He longs to do so because He loves you so. The locusts may have eaten for a bit…but God will restore all that has been taken and the harvest will be abundant once again.

Question of the day: What have the locusts eaten in your life?

Quote of the day: "Everything that the enemy has stolen, God is going to restore: the joy, the peace, the health, the dreams…" Unknown

Prayer: Lord, You know all of the things that the locusts have stolen from me, they were not hidden from You. I rest in Your promise to restore what has been stolen, lost, or eaten. I believe in Your ability to do so and I am humbled that You would bestow such a kindness to me. Thank You and I pray this in the Name that restores all things, Jesus, Amen.


Further Scripture Reading

Isaiah 61:7

1 Peter 5:10

# Day 85

"I have been crucified with Christ and I no longer live, but Christ lives in me. The life I now live in the body, I live by faith in the Son of God, who loved me and gave himself for me." Galatians 2:20

Have you noticed that this world has created people who are easily offended? Just about *everything* offends *someone*. I heard a quote a few years ago that I wish I hadn't heard…because it convicted my heart, right to the core. The quote said, "Dead men don't get offended." What? When I dove into the meaning of this quote, I realized that it had the power to change my perspective and in doing so, change my life. Dead men don't get offended. When I asked Christ to come into my life, I became crucified with Him. I no longer live, but Jesus Christ lives in me. I am dead. Dead to flesh. Dead to the things of the world. Dead to self. Dead. And dead men don't get offended. This changed the way I looked at what other people said about me, their likes and dislikes, or their opinion that differ with mine. When something is said or done that offends me, I stop and remember this quote and it quickly releases me from my right to get offended. It relinquishes my entitlement to be hurt or upset because let's face it, most of the time when we are offended, it is nothing of significant consequence. It may be a matter of perspective or a personal preference but nothing of a great magnitude. If you are not careful, you can waste precious time walking the path of being easily offended. It will capture your time. Drain your energy. Redirect your focus. All for what? Just so you can say that you were offended? Ya'll…it's time that we recognize that being easily offended is not how we should live…it is how we should die…die to ourselves…die to our flesh…die to our "rights". Is it hard living "dead"? Yes, sometimes. Is it worth living "dead"? Yes, always. Do yourself a favor and live "dead"…because dead men don't get offended.

Question of the day: What does the phrase, "Dead men don't get offended" mean to you?

Quote of the day: "An offended heart is the breeding ground of deception." John Bevere

Prayer: Lord, I confess that at times I can be easily offended. Remind me that I was crucified with Christ and I no longer live. I ask that You show me how to overlook any offense that comes my way. Dead men don't get offended. Help me to see the wisdom in that statement, Lord. I believe You for it, I trust You for it, in Jesus Name, Amen.

Further Scripture Reading:

Proverbs 19:11

Colossians 2:20

# Day 86

"What sorrow for those who drag their sins behind them with ropes made of lies, who drag wickedness behind them like a cart!" Isaiah 5:18 (NLT)

My husband and I were recently taking a trip and were carrying our luggage through the airport. Well, carrying isn't really the correct term. Lindsey had that really cool luggage that had four wheels and he could push, pull, and cart it quite easily. But not me. Nope. I had bought my luggage at Goodwill and it only had two wheels. The faster we walked the more wonky my luggage got. It would teeter from one side to the other...much like a Weeble Wobble. So imagine me with my Weebly Wobbly luggage along with my carry-on trying to get to our terminal...it was quite a sight. Maybe you look like me too...not in the airport but in life. You struggle getting over the things in your past. Some of them were mistakes, some of them were sin. Both still haunt you. You can't shake it. You can't gloss over it. You can't forgive it and you certainly can't forget it. It's like luggage that you drag behind you everywhere you go. That baggage is a pain to cart everywhere you go but you don't really know what else to do with it. So, you drag it, roll it, weave it in and out of places. You bump into it. It rolls over your toes. It makes you tired, and frustrated, and sad. This, my baggage-lugging-friend, is what Isaiah 5:18 is talking about. What sorrow indeed! The ropes you are holding on to are made of lies, pure lies. The baggage you are dragging behind you brings you sorrow but you keep holding on to that rope, dragging and carting the past around. So, how are you supposed to just "forget" all of the things you are the most ashamed about? How do you stop worrying about what you've done? First, drop the rope. Yep, drop it like it's hot. After you drop the rope of lies that is attached to your baggage, do what Isaiah 43:18 says; "Forget the former things; do not dwell on the past." Why should you forget? Because God does, that's why! "For I will forgive their wickedness and will remember their sins no more." Hebrews 8:12. I remember hearing a radio preacher talk about how God forgets our sins. I loved his perspective on it. He said that God doesn't "forget" our sins because He's forgetful or because He has long-term memory loss or even because He just can't remember our sins. It's because He chooses not to. He CHOOSES not to remember our sins any more. He made a choice to not remember. It's His choice and you have to make it yours too. Drop the rope.

Question of the day: Do you drag your past around like baggage and if so, what lies are attached to it?

Quote of the day: "You can't reach for anything new if your hands are still full of yesterday's junk." Louise Smith

Prayer: Lord, I confess that I have been dragging around my past sins and mistakes. It has hindered me and my walk with You. I am ready to drop the rope. Thank You for how You see me. I love you. I pray this in Jesus Name, Amen.

Further Scripture Reading:

Philippians 3:13

2 Corinthians 5:17-18

Worship: Clean by Natalie Grant

# Day 87

"Together they will be like warriors in battle trampling their enemy into the mud of the streets. They will fight because the LORD is with them, and they will put the enemy horsemen to shame."
Zechariah 10:5

"Wakanda forever!"…this phrase along with the well-known hand motions are from the blockbuster hit, <u>Black Panther</u>. Marvel released this film in February of 2018 and it was ranked the 12th highest grossing movie of all-time (worldwide). The premise of the story is that after the death of his father, T'Challa returns home to the African nation of Wakanda to take his rightful place as king. When a powerful enemy suddenly reappears, T'Challa's mettle as king -- and as Black Panther -- gets tested when he's drawn into a conflict that puts the fate of Wakanda and the entire world at risk. Faced with treachery and danger, the young king must rally his allies and release the full power of Black Panther to defeat his foes and secure the safety of his people. Our entire family LOVED this movie and I, for one, wanted to be a Wakandan Warrior. The fight scenes and the battles were especially epic. Could you see yourself in one of those battles? Could you see yourself defending Wakanda as a mighty warrior? That idea may seem ridiculous to you. You, a warrior? Well, actually you are…not for Wakanda, but for the Kingdom of God. As a warrior, you will battle many things. You will face many wars. There are times you will be asked by God to go in and conquer…and you need to believe that you can. Other times, you need to stand firm and let God do the fighting for you. Not every battle is yours but every victory is His. There is a balance to being a mighty warrior. A warrior always takes direction from his/her king. Sometimes the king may want the warrior to go into the battle, swords raised, and conquer the enemy. Sometimes the king may ask the warrior to guard over something important instead of doing the fighting. There may be times where the king tells the warrior, "This isn't your battle to fight. Sit this one out." Whatever is asked of the warrior, he/she does so, trusting the king. It's no different when you are a warrior for Christ. You just have to be ready and willing to hear what your King is asking…which part of "Warrior" is He asking of you. Fight? Guard? Be still? You can trust your King...for there is no greater Warrior. Wakanda forever!

Question of the day: Are you a warrior?

Quote of the day: "The true soldier fights not because he hates what is in front of him, but because he loves what is behind him." G.K. Chesterton

Prayer: Lord, You have called me to be a Warrior and I will fight for You. Help my heart to be tuned in to how You want me to fight. You are my King and always victorious. Thank You Lord and I pray this in Jesus Name, Amen.

Further Scripture Reading:

Ephesians 6:10-18

# Day 88

"…because judgment without mercy will be shown to anyone who has not been merciful. Mercy triumphs over judgment." James 2:13

I was pulled out of bed early one morning. It wasn't my bed though, it was another man's bed. I knew I was in trouble. The men from the church drug me from the house and I was pretty sure I knew what was going to happen next. I was going to die. I lowered my head and tears fell uncontrollably. I finally looked up and realized I was in a church, facing a young man who I didn't know. I stole a glance around the room and there were many men standing around, all with smirks on their faces. *I* was their entertainment. The men who had brought me there said to the young man, "Teacher, this woman was caught in adultery. The Law says we are to stone her. What do you say?" Teacher? So he's a Teacher. Great. I'm definitely going to die. The Teacher looked at me, eyes tender and full of…I don't really know what it was…love maybe? That's strange because he doesn't even know me. Anyway, I held my breath, waiting for his answer. But he didn't. He didn't answer. Instead, he leaned down and wrote something in the dirt. I was too ashamed and embarrassed to look so I just kept standing there. The teacher straightened up and then said, "If any of you is without sin, let him be the first to throw a stone at her." I felt my body become tense as I closed my eyes. I didn't want to see the stones coming. All of a sudden, I heard a thud. Followed by another one. And another one. What *was* that sound? I finally found the courage to open my eyes and saw a pile of rocks where the men once stood. Gone. All of them were gone. The Teacher looked at me and asked, "Where are they? Has no one condemned you?" I couldn't believe what I was seeing or hearing. I stuttered, "No one, sir." And then the Teacher said something I will never, ever forget. He said, "Then neither do I condemn you. Go now and leave your life of sin." What once felt like a noose around my neck, now felt like a row of diamonds and jewels. What once felt like a death sentence, now felt like the wings of freedom. All because of this one Teacher.

Ya'll, this is what it looks like when *mercy* triumphs over *judgement.* You can be like the Pharisees…pointing out people's sin. You can be like the bystanders…waiting to throw a rock in judgement. Or, you can be like Jesus…the Mercy-Giver. You might be thinking, "Well, what about the woman? What if you are like her?"

Beloved, we are **ALL** like that woman. Every.single.one.of.us.

Question of the day: What does mercy triumphing over judgement mean to you and how do you see it played out in this story?

Quote of the day: "Mercy imitates God and disappoints Satan." John Chrysotom

Prayer: Oh God, how I've missed it! How I've missed the outpouring of mercy. I get so caught up in the judgement of others that I have completely forgotten about mercy. The mercy You have shown me is so underserved yet I don't bestow that same mercy on others. Please forgive me. Help me to be a Mercy-Giver instead of a Judgement-Maker. I ask this in Your Son's precious Name, Jesus, Amen.

Further Scripture Reading:

John 8:1-11

# Day 89

"But the Lord stood at my side and gave me strength, so that through me the message might be fully proclaimed and all the Gentiles might hear it. And I was delivered from the lion's mouth." 2 Timothy 4:17

When our kids were little we would vacation in North Carolina. We made it a habit to stop in South Carolina and take the kids to the zoo that was there. I'm not actually sure who had the most fun, us or the kids! One of my favorite exhibits to see is the lions. They are so majestic and mighty. I've always wanted to just stick my hand in there and pet their mane or scratch them behind the ear like a kitten but one look at those big 'ol teeth and it's apparent why there is a "Do not enter" sign on their cage. I can't look at a lion without thinking about the story of Daniel. Daniel was a man who loved God and made no bones about it. He defied the king's order not to worship anyone other than the king. He worshiped God anyway and was thrown into a den of lions. Hungry lions. God sent an angel to shut the mouths of the lions and Daniel did not have a single mark on him the next morning. The Lord was with David and *He* took care of the lions. You may be going through a situation where you feel like the lions are about to devour you. Maybe it's a family situation or a circumstance at your job. You might feel like people are out to get you. Maybe they are running their mouths about you, spreading lies. Maybe you are successful and people around you don't like it so they are making it impossible for you. Maybe you are trying to do the right thing but junk just keeps getting thrown your way. Lions. Here's what I know. The Lord is standing at your side, giving you strength and He will deliver you from the lion's mouth. He created the lions so He knows how to handle them. You aren't in charge of the lions just like Daniel wasn't. God is. Leave it to Him. Now, I don't know how He shut those lions up but in reality, I don't care, I'm just thankful He did. When I have had situations arise in my life where people are after my character or talking about me, I pray one simple prayer and maybe you can pray it too. "Lord, shut the mouths of the lions." And do you know what? He always does. He's the best lion tamer in history.

Question of the day: Have you ever had an experience with those types of "lions"? What will you do from now on when faced with those lions?

Quote of the day: "He [God] is the best lion tamer in history." Karen Mutchler Allen

Prayer: God, thank You for shutting the mouths of the lions when they are seeking to devour me. I trust You with every situation that happens in my life where I need You to step in and tame a lion. Thank You for all the times You have stepped in and all the times You will step in and save me in the lion's den. I love and trust You, in Jesus Name, Amen.

Further Scripture Reading:

Daniel 6

# Day 90

"Come near to God and he will come near to you."
James 4:8

When our son was a toddler and would start getting sleepy, he would begin to whine as most little ones do. I would say, "Come here to me!" as I held out my arms. He would waddle towards me with outstretched arms and I'd swoop him up and hold him until he fell asleep. Listen. Do you hear that? Do you hear the whisper of your Abba? He is saying the same to you, Beloved. "Come here to me!" His arms are outstretched, waiting to hold you. For the last ninety days, you've drawn near to God. You've come close. Leaned in. Listened. Talked. Cried out. Grown. As you have drawn near to God through spending time with Him, He has delighted in you just as a parent delights in spending time with their child. This is what taking a "Selah" is all about. A pause. A pause with a purpose. Ninety days of pauses for the purpose of inhaling, exhaling, and taking a moment to stop in this crazy, busy world. You are *worth* the pause. Your spirit *needs* this pause. Keep pressing in to Him. Keep drawing close.

Don't stop.  He is your lifeline, your oxygen, your breath.  When you treat your "Selah" with that focus, how could you NOT spend time with Him?  Oh how He loves you, Beloved.  Oh how He cherishes His time with you.  He continues to hold open His arms and whisper, "Come here to me!"

Question of the day:  How has this devotional book helped you with your "Selah"?

Quote of the day:  "We never grow closer to God when we just live life. It takes deliberate pursuit and attentiveness."  Francis Chan

Prayer:  Lord, thank You for drawing close to me as I intentionally have been drawing close to You.  I need You.  I need time with You.  I need to speak to You and I need to hear You speak to me.  My heart is Yours and so is my life.  I love You more than I can find the words to express.  Thank You for loving me the way You do.  I pray this in Jesus Name, Amen.

Further Scripture Reading:

Psalm 145:18

Hebrews 4:16


Worship:  Draw Near by Bethel Worship

# Notes

"With the new day comes new strength and new thoughts." Eleanor Roosevelt/brainyquote.com

"Suffering has been stronger than all other teaching, and has taught me to understand what your heart used to be. I have been bent and broken, but – I hope – into a better shape." Charles Dickens /Goodreads.com

"Being different and thinking differently make a person unforgettable. History does not remember the forgettable. It honors the unique minority the majority cannot forget." Suzy Kassem, /Goodreads.com

"Biblically, waiting is not just something we have to do until we get what we want. Waiting is part of the process of becoming what God wants us to be." John Ortberg/Wiseoldsayings.com

"The Church exists for nothing else but to draw men into Christ, to make them little Christs. If they are not doing that, all the cathedrals, clergy, missions, sermons, even the Bible itself, are simply a waste of time. God became Man for no other purpose." C.S. Lewis /azquotes.com

"The ability of a person to atone has always been the most remarkable of human features." Leon Uris/keepinspiring.me

"God bestows His blessings without discrimination." F.F. Bruce/ ChristianQuotes.info

"An unintentional life accepts everything and does nothing.  An intentional life embraces only the things that will add to the mission of significance." John C Maxell/simpleandsoul.com

"God is God.  Because he is God, He is worthy of my trust and obedience.  I will find rest nowhere but in His holy will that is unspeakably beyond my largest notions of what he is up to." Elisabeth Elliot/goodreads.com

"Rest time is not waste time.  It is economy to gather fresh strength…It is wisdom to take occasional furlough.  In the long run, we shall do more by sometimes doing less." Charles Spurgeon /Christianquotes.info

"Handle them carefully, for words have more power than atom bombs." Pearl Strachan Hurd/ inc.com

"Surround yourself with the dreamers, and the doers, the believers, and thinkers, but most of all, surround yourself with those who see the greatness within you, even when you don't see it yourself." Edmund Lee/awakenthegreatnesswithin.com

"If you want to discover the true character of a person, you have only to observe what they are passionate about." Shannon L. Alder/goodreads.com

"It is the Holy Spirit's job to convict, God's job to judge and my job to love." Billy Graham/goodreads.com

"He touched me, Oh He touched me, And oh the joy that floods my soul! Something happened and now I know, He touched me and made me whole." Bill Gaither/Lyrics.com

"Lazarus, come out!" John 11:43

"Don't love to be loved in return. Love for the sake of loving." Connor Chalfant/goodreads.com

"Everyone has the potential to become an encourager. You don't have to be rich. You don't have to be a genius.

You don't have to have it all together. All you have to do is care about people and initiate." John C. Maxwell/azquotes.com

"You have never truly found Jesus if you do not tell others about Him!" Charles Spurgeon/Crosswalk.com

"He that won't be counseled can't be helped." Benjamin Franklin/brainyquote.com

"Time can be an ally or an enemy. What it becomes depends entirely upon you, your goals, and your determination to use every available minute." Zig Ziglar/motivationgrid.com

"We all face storms in life. Some are more difficult than others, but we all go through trials and tribulation. That's why we have the gift of faith." Joyce Meyer/brainyquotes.com

"Does the sheep need to know how to use a complicated sextant to calculate its coordinates? Does it need to be able to use a GPS to define its position? Does it have to have the expertise to create an app that will call for help? Does the sheep need endorsements by a sponsor before the Good Shepherd will come to the rescue? No. Certainly not! The sheep is worthy of divine rescue simply because it is loved by the Good Shepherd." Dieter F. Uchtdorf /ids.org

Laughter is poison to fear." George R.R.Martin/ biblereasons.com

"As you walk through the valley of the unknown, you will find the footprints of Jesus both in front of you and beside you." Charles Stanley/pinterest.com

"The greatest honor is the right direction one is turned into by the Holy Spirit." Sunday Adelaja/goodreads.com

"Our love is unconditional, we knew it from the start. I can see it in your eyes, you can feel it from my heart." Pure Country/I Cross my Heart/Youtube.com

"Though our feelings come and go, God's love for us does not." C.S. Lewis/Christianquotes.info

"We must remember there are different seasons in our lives and let God do what He wants to do in each of those seasons"./Joyce Meyers, *from Be Anxious for Nothing: The Art of Casting Your Cares and Resting in God*

"Preach the Gospel at all times. When necessary, use words." St. Francis of Assisi/goodreads.com

"Hagar's God is the One who numbers the hairs on our heads and who knows our circumstances, past, present, and future. When you pray to El Roi, you are praying to the one who knows everything about you." Ann Spangler/Crosswalk.com

"Trying to please others before pleasing God is inverting the first and second great commandments." Lynn G. Robbins/goodreads.com

"And like an echo, God often uses the repetitive events and themes in daily life to get my attention and draw me closer to himself." Margaret Feinberg/goodreads.com

"No act of kindness, no matter how small, is ever wasted." Aesop/brainyquote.com/topics/kindness

"No matter what our circumstances, we can find a reason to be thankful." Dr. David Jeremiah/crosswalk.com

"God's strength in your weakness is His presence in your life." Andy Stanley/countingmyblessings.com

"Fear defeats more people than any other one thing in the world." Ralph Waldo Emerson/mantelligence.com

"God pursues us for the purpose of a redemptive relationship." Dr. Gary Fenton/Pinterest.com

"No behavior on our part is more self-centered than the demand to speak and the refusal to listen." Robert E. Fisher/goodreads.com

"Your heart needs to worship every day. Actually, your heart WILL worship every day. You get to decide what your heart will worship." marcalanschelske.com/you-have-idols/

"When anything in life is an absolute requirement for your happiness and self-worth, it is essentially an 'idol,' something you are actually worshiping. When such a thing is threatened, your anger is absolute. Your anger is actually the way the idol keeps you in its service, in its chains." Tim Keller/christianquotes.com

"Wearing a mask wears you out. Faking it is fatiguing. The most exhausting activity is pretending to be what you know you aren't." Rick Warren/azquotes.com

"The two most important days in your life are the day you were born and the day you find out why." Mark Twain/goodreads.com

"To holy people the very name of Jesus is a name to feed upon, a name to transport. His name can raise the dead and transfigure and beautify the living." John Henry Newman/azquotes.com

"He's still working on me" by Joel Hemphill/gospelfamily.org

"I am currently under construction.  Thank you for your patience."  Pinterest


"Jesus came to save us:  let us not reject this marvelous gift!"  Pope Francis/picturequotes.com


"Ninety percent of all human wisdom is the ability to mind your own business." Robert A. Heinlein/azquotes.com


"Never, never, never give up."  Winston Churchill/quote/coyote.com


"When we get to the end of our life, the question playing over and over in our mind will be, "Did my life make a difference?" Brian Fleming/wow4u.com


"You do not have to be special, but you have to be available."  Winkie Pratney/christianquotes.com


"I've got the joy" lyrics/childbiblesongs.com

"Joy is distinctly a Christian word and a Christian thing. It is the reverse of happiness. Happiness is the result of what happens of an agreeable sort. Joy has its springs deep down inside. And that spring never runs dry, no matter what happens. Only Jesus gives that joy. He had joy, singing its music within, even under the shadow of the cross." S.D. Gordon

"Green means growth and I had always felt I had to be up and moving in order to be growing. Once I was "made" to lie down, I learned that having the opportunity to stop and ponder and pray and ask for understanding, were my green pastures of growth." Darla Isackson/ldsmag.com/article-1-8278/

"We didn't tackle well today but we made up for it by not blocking." John McKay, Coach for Tampa Bay Buccaneers/sportsfeelgoodstories.com

"The way we love the people we don't agree with, is the best evidence that the tomb is really empty." Bob Goff/twitter.com

"But even if He does not. That is slowly where God is moving me and how I long to respond as I face every giant crisis: knowing He is able to do all, but even if He does not, my faith will not waiver. We can't answer all the whys. We can't possibly grasp what His "good" is. But we can choose to be steadfast, even if we don't get what we want. Our circumstances don't change His character and the truth about who He is." Emily Roberts/inheritanceofhope.org

"If I find in myself desires which nothing in this world can satisfy, the only logical explanation is that I was made for another world." C.S. Lewis/goodreads.com

"God never gives up on us—but tragically, all too often we give up on God!" Billy Graham/BillyGraham.org

"The worship to which we are called in our renewed state is far too important to be left to personal preferences, to whims, or to marketing strategies. It is the pleasing of God that is at the heart of worship. Therefore, our worship must be informed at every point by the Word of God as we seek God's own instructions for worship that is pleasing to Him." R.C. Sproul/mediashout.com

"There is no doubt that it is around the family and the home that all the greatest virtues, the most dominating virtues of human, are created, strengthened and maintained." Winston S. Churchill/goodreads.com

"If we do not abide in prayer, we will abide in temptation. Let this be one aspect of our daily intercession: "God, preserve my soul, and keep my heart and all its ways so that I will not be entangled." When this is true in our lives, a passing temptation will not overcome us. We will remain free while others lie in bondage." John Owen/christian-quotes.ochristian.com

"If you've asked God for answers but find yourself waiting longer than you planned, take a moment now to thank Him in advance for His answer. Trust that He is working behind the scenes on your behalf. Don't give up. Look forward in hope and expectancy for Him to respond and remember that the Lord is good to those who seek Him." Leah DiPascal/Proverbs31.org

"The things you do when no one's looking are the things that define you."
Anonymous/awakenthegreatnesswithin.com

"The naysayers of the day, the religious aristocracy, criticized Jesus as a "glutton and a drunkard, a friend of tax collectors and sinners." They called him this because it was true. He was a friend of sinners." Jonathan Parnell/desiringGod.org

"God uses imperfect people who are in imperfect situations to do His perfect will." David Young/Pinterest.com

"Shut the world out, withdraw from all worldly thoughts and occupations, and shut yourself in alone with God, to pray to Him in secret. Let this be your chief object in prayer, to realize the presence of your heavenly Father." Andy Murray/onethingalone.com

"God is writing your story. Stop trying to steal the pen." Unknown/pinterest.com

"If anybody understands God's ardor for his children, it's someone who has rescued an orphan from despair, for that is what God has done for us. God has adopted you. God sought you, found you, signed the papers and took you home." Max Lucado/whatchristianswanttoknow.com

"Love that goes upward is worship; Love that goes outward is affection; Love that stoops is grace." Donald Barnhouse/azquotes.com

"Live free or die: Death is not the worst of evils." General John Stark/quoteambition.com

"Words are like eggs dropped from great heights; you can no more call them back than ignore the mess they leave when they fall." Jodi Picoult/goodreads.com

"Consider how hard it is to change yourself and you'll understand what little chance you have in trying to change others." Jacob M. Braude/goodreads.com

"One person at a time, one day at a time, and one project at a time, you can make a difference that will leave a lasting impact on the world." Asad Meah/awakenthegreatnesswithin.com

"On earth we have nothing to do with success or its results, but only being true to God and for God; for it is sincerity and not success which is the sweet savor before God." Frederick W. Robertson/christianquotes.com

"Never be afraid to trust an unknown future to a known God." Corrie Ten Boom/jonbeaty.com

"Getting out of the boat was Peter's great gift to Jesus; the experience of walking on water was Jesus' great gift to Peter." John Ortburg/faithgateway.com

"A word from Jesus changed everything." Henry T. Blackaby /goodreads.com

"A true friend unbosoms freely, advises justly, assists readily, adventures boldly, takes all patiently, defends courageously, and continues a friend unchangeably." William Penn/goodreads.com

"Fall seven times. Stand up eight." Japanese Proverb/goodreads.com

"When your temper becomes frayed, your sensibility is in shreds." Anthony T. Hincks/goodreads.com

"An offended heart is the breeding ground of deception." John Bevere/golfian.com

en.wikipedia.org/wiki/Locust

You can't reach for anything new if your hands are still full of yesterday's junk." Louise Smith/wiseoldsayings.com

"The true soldier fights not because he hates what is in front of him, but because he loves what is behind him." G.K. Chesterton/quotabulary.com

Mercy imitates God and disappoints Satan." John Chrysotom/ viralbeliever.com

"We never grow closer to God when we just live life. It takes deliberate pursuit and attentiveness." Francis Chan/goodreads.com

# Other books written by Karen Mutchler Allen

Children's Books

The Couth Fairy

The Couth Fairy Returns

The Couth Fairy Goes to School

The Awesome Opossum

Other Selections

The One:  In the search for my husband I found my Father

Little Miss Less-Than-Perfect:  Why women dabble in the art of comparison

You can purchase these books at Amazon.com or visit Karen's website at **Karenallen.weebly.com**

36640868R00165

Made in the USA
Columbia, SC
26 November 2018